God
in the
Hard
Times

Dale Evans Rogers

with
Floyd Thatcher

WORD BOOKS
PUBLISHER
WACO, TEXAS

A DIVISION OF
WORD, INCORPORATED

GOD IN THE HARD TIMES

Scripture quotations in this publication are from the
following sources:
    The Jerusalem Bible (JB), copyright © 1966, by Darton,
Longman & Todd. Ltd. and Doubleday and Company, Inc.
    The King James Version of the Bible (KJV).
    *The Modern Language Bible: The New Berkeley Version in
Modern English* (MLB), copyright © 1945, 1959, 1969 by
Zondervan Publishing House.
    The New International Version of the Bible (NIV),
published by the Zondervan Corporation, copyright © 1978
by the New York International Bible Society.
    The New King James Bible—New Testament (NKJV),
copyright © 1979, by Thomas Nelson, Inc., Publishers.
    The New Testament in Modern English (PHILLIPS), copyright
© 1958, 1960, 1972 by J.B. Phillips.
    The Revised Standard Version of the Bible (RSV), copyright
© 1946, 1952, © 1971 and 1973 by the Division of Christian
Education of the National Council of the Churches of Christ
in the U.S.A.
    The Acts of the Apostles by C.H. Rieu (C.H. RIEU), copyright
© 1957 by Penguin Books, Ltd.
    The *Good News Bible*, the Bible in Today's English Version
(TEV). Copyright © American Bible Society, 1976.

Library of Congress Cataloging in Publication Data

Rogers, Dale Evans.
    God in the hard times.

    Includes bibliographical references.
    1. Suffering—Religious aspects—Christianity.
2. Consolation. 3. Rogers, Dale Evans. I. Thatcher,
Floyd W. II. Title.
BV4909.R64 1984   248.8'6   84-13002
ISBN 0-8499-0343-2

Contents

1. God in the Hard Times   7

2. God in the Hard Times of Disappointment   19

3. God in the Hard Times of Loneliness   37

4. God in the Hard Times of Failure   57

5. God in the Hard Times of Temptation   75

6. God in the Hard Times of Success   93

7. God in the Hard Times of Marriage   111

8. God in the Hard Times of Death   129

About the Authors   143

Notes   145

God in the Hard Times   1.

---

*"One of the great paradoxes of the
Christian faith is that we learn through
difficulties and hard times. Yet we
resist them in our passion to live safely
and avoid hurt."*

*"Though I live surrounded by trouble,
you keep me alive . . .
You stretch your hand out and save me,
your right hand will do everything for me."*

Psalm 138:7–8, JB

"IN CAMBRIDGE there is nothing so troublesome as that one has nothing to trouble one."

So spoke Thomas Gray, a gifted British poet, many years ago. Imagine! This very wise and talented man felt troubled because everything seemed to be running smoothly, and he wasn't experiencing any hard times. There were no disturbances or reverses in his life, and he was upset about it.

Does that seem unreal in these stressful and fast-moving days of the 1980s? Of course it does. And I suspect it was unreal even back in Thomas Gray's day for most people. We know that men and women have been plagued by hard times since that infamous day in the Garden of Eden when Adam and

Eve sinned against God and hid from him because of their shame and disobedience and nakedness.

An unreal longing

And yet there is something about those words from Gray that ignites a longing in most of our hearts. In our humanness we long for an earthly existence that is free from times of pain and hurt and anxiety. So often we cry out in anger and rebellion when things, as we understand them, don't turn out right or the way we want them to. And we exert enormous time and energy in an effort to insulate ourselves against life's hard places. Why, I've even known people who refused to become involved on an intimate level with friends for fear of being disappointed and getting hurt.

But Henri Nouwen, one of the most perceptive Christians of our time, peels back the layers of our insulation with these words, "To wait for moments or places where no pain exists, no separation is felt and where all human restlessness has turned into inner peace is waiting for a dream world."[1] And I know from long experience there is no dream world out there anywhere. Ours is a real world—a world of broken relationships . . . of loneliness . . . of disappointment . . . of being misunderstood . . . of sickness and death . . . of hunger and poverty . . . of suspicion and war and terrorism.

Thank God, though, there is an antidote to the hard times that plague us in this "real world"—and that is Jesus Christ. Through him we can overcome, even though the Enemy of our souls will use every trick in the book to defeat us, to get us to give in to despair and hopelessness. And it's easy to feel discouraged and defeated when we read our daily newspaper and watch the six o'clock news on television.

But again, that is only part of the story. A truth we seem to forget so easily is that Satan was defeated at Calvary on that climactic first Easter morning. It was that momentous event that makes us Resurrection Christians in our hard times as well as in our good times. And it is Resurrection Christians who have the heart to draw on the divine resources that are ours and move ahead boldly in the midst of life's risks and dangers in our pilgrimage toward growth and maturity in the Christian walk.

The payoff for hard times

One of the great paradoxes of the Christian faith is that we learn and grow through difficulties and hard times. Yet we resist them in our passion to live safely and avoid hurt. But Bernard Baruch, a wise and brilliant counselor to several United States presidents, cut through so much of the superficial thinking of his day and ours with this perceptive comment, "The art of living lies not in eliminating but in growing with troubles." And a great Jewish thinker has given us this profound sentence, "Mature people are not made out of good times but out of bad times." I'd like to suggest that you take those two statements and write them out on a small card that can be tucked into the corner of your mirror where you can see them every morning. These are attitude-changers that can give new meaning and understanding and zest to life.

Jeremy Taylor, that great eighteenth-century man of God, said on one occasion, "It is usually not so much the greatness of our trouble as the littleness of our spirit which makes us complain." I think he hit on something very important for each of us. The Christian life has always called for us to be people with "bigness of spirit." After all, it is "bigness of spirit" that will help us handle life's rough places and hard times. It is this spirit that will give us the capability to be "more than conquerors through him that loved us" (Rom. 8:37, KJV). And it is this spirit that will give us the strength and power to handle adversity, to risk and face danger in the name of Jesus, and to grow and mature in our Christian walk.

Stevenson's secret

Robert Louis Stevenson was without a doubt one of our greatest American authors. He was a magnificent storyteller. Few writers in history have had Stevenson's ability to manipulate words in such a colorful fashion. But he was on intimate terms with hard times. At one point in his career he was so poor he couldn't afford to pay the few dollars a month rent that his house in Calistoga, California, cost him. So he prepared to take his young wife and child and move to an abandoned bunkhouse in the deserted Silverado mine. It was a time of desperation and humiliation. Yet, this is what he wrote on his last night before leaving picturesque Calistoga: "I have never seen such a night. . . . The sky itself was of a ruddy, powerful, nameless, changing color, dark and glossy like a serpent's back. The stars by innumerable millions stuck boldly forth like lamps. The Milky Way was bright, like a moonlit cloud; half heaven seemed Milky Way."

There's no sound of defeat evident in his struggle to cope with difficulties, no smell of complaint in the midst of adversity. In one of his sermons Dr. Norman Vincent Peale speaks of Stevenson and the illnesses that plagued him all his life. Dr. Peale points out that Stevenson was a happy man in spite of illness and tells how one morning Mrs. Stevenson said to him, "Robert, I don't understand how you can be so happy."

Stevenson glanced over at the assortment of medicine bottles that lined the shelf in his room, and said, "My dear, I'll have you know that I'm not going to let my life be regulated by a row of medicine bottles."

The risk and the secret

There's a hint here in Stevenson's words of the spirit of the Apostle Paul when he recounted some of his hard times: five times he received thirty-nine lashes from the Jewish authorities, three times he endured a beating with rods, and once he was stoned. On three different occasions he was shipwrecked and one of those times he drifted at sea for a day and a night. Then he speaks of "perils of waters, in perils of robbers, in perils of mine own countrymen . . . in perils in the city, in perils in the wilderness . . ." Talk about trouble and hard times; this man had them! But it was also Paul who wrote, "I believe nothing can happen that will outweigh the supreme advantage of knowing Christ Jesus my Lord. For him I have accepted the loss of everything, and I look on everything as so much rubbish if only I can have Christ and be given a place in him" (Phil. 3:8–9, JB). Here, indeed, is our model for a spirit and attitude that will give victory over adversity.

In George Bernard Shaw's play *Saint Joan* we find a powerful statement about the risk and danger that goes with being a Christian. Before sentence is passed on Joan of Arc, Bishop Cauchin says to her, "My child, you are in love with religion." Joan asks, "I never thought of that. Is there any harm in it?" The bishop answers, "No, my child. There is no harm in it. But there is danger."

While today there are those in Third World countries and in the Middle East who suffer physical dangers for their faith, we in the Western world are not usually confronted with physical "perils" as such. But if we live boldly for Jesus Christ, we will confront a host of emotional and spiritual dangers that are very real. Whatever the dangers and hard times, we can rest confident that our God will, if we are open to him, carry us through every difficulty.

When Dr. James B. Conant was President of Harvard University, he kept on his desk a little model of a turtle with this inscription, "Consider the turtle. It makes progress only when it sticks its neck out." Yes, that is an old and homey maxim, but there is a world of rich truth in it. We grow and mature by risking for God even in our hard times. And as we grow, old experiences and old truths become new— life takes on adventure. We can move ahead with confidence in Paul's promise, "If any one is in Christ, he is a new creation; the old has passed away, behold, the new has come" (2 Cor. 5:17, RSV).

The Habakkuk story

There is an obscure and unsung hero in the Old Testament that I wish we knew more about. His name is Habakkuk. Very little is known about this deeply troubled man, but evidently he lived in Judah between five and six hundred years before Christ. It is quite likely that Habakkuk saw his country plundered first by the armies of Egypt, and then some years later young Nebuchadnezzar of Babylon overran Egypt and moved up north and east to conquer Judah. These were desperate days; human life was cheap and slavery was commonplace—times were unbelievably hard. It took a lot of nerve to stand up and be counted in those days, so I have to believe that Habakkuk was a pretty crusty and intrepid man.

We first meet Habakkuk as he cries out in agony to God about the dreadful conditions in Judah—violence threatens survival, and God doesn't seem to be doing anything about it . . . strife and evil and plundering are tearing the nation apart and inflicting horrible suffering on the people . . . there's no law and order . . . wickedness prevails and justice has disappeared . . . God seems deaf to Habakkuk's prayers and indifferent to the hard times of the Jewish people.

These were the worst of days—the midnight hours of the soul. But this rugged prophet held on to God until he received words of promise and hope. There are only three chapters in this short book—fifty-six verses in all. But out of the gloom and seeming doom of those times came the electrifying words, "The just shall live by faith"—*by being faithful.* The Apostle Paul picked up on this theme when he, too, wrote, "The just shall live by faith" (Rom. 1:17, KJV). And thousands of years later Habakkuk's pronouncement launched the Reformation when these same words became Martin Luther's battle cry as he moved to free the church from the decadence of the times.

But that isn't all. We have Habakkuk to thank for two other memorable statements that have lived throughout the centuries: ". . . the Lord is in His holy temple. Let all the earth keep silence before Him" and ". . . I will rejoice in the Lord, I will joy in the God of my salvation. The Lord God is my strength; He will make my feet like deer's *feet,* and He will make me walk on my high hills" (Hab. 2:20 and 3:18–19, NKJV). And these optimistic words were written while trouble hovered over Habakkuk and Judah like a dark thunder cloud!

As I've thought about writing this book, I have been driven again and again to the Bible stories and the rugged Bible characters found in them. And it is here that I have discovered flesh and blood examples which can give us hope and encouragement and direction as we try to cope with our hard times. I can testify personally to a truth about these stories that was so well expressed by Anne Morrow Lindberg, author of the classic *Gift from the Sea:* "They are so simple that they are like empty cups for people to fill with their own experience and drink for their own need over and over again, through the years." For this reason, in the chapters that follow in which we turn our attention to specific hard times that come to all of us in our human pilgrimage, I will be turning to the experiences of many characters in the Bible drama as examples of how we, you and I, can handle our hard times.

The good news

And we *will* have hard times, but the good news is that they don't have to swamp us. I know from experience that our hope and strength lie in the words of the third verse of Faber's magnificent hymn, "There's a Wideness in God's Mercy":

> For the love of God is broader
>   Than the measure of man's mind;
> And the heart of the Eternal
>   Is most wonderfully kind.
> If our love were but more simple,
>   We should take him at his word;
> And our loves would be all sunshine
>   In the sweetness of the Lord.

God in the Hard Times
of Disappointment 2.

---

*"For the Christian, disappointments
are opportunities to learn more of
Christ and his will for our lives. And it
is in our disappointments that we learn
to live out the words, 'And we know
that in all things God works for the
good of those who love him . . .'"*
(Rom. 8:28, NIV)

"Don't throw away your trust now—it carries with it a rich reward. Patient endurance is what you need if, after doing God's will, you are to receive what he has promised."

Hebrews 10:35–36, PHILLIPS

_____

IN ONE OF JEAN KERR'S delightful books she tells the story of the little boy who came home from school and announced to his mother that the teacher had selected him to play a part in a class play based on creation.

When his mother asked what part he had been given, he answered, "Adam."

Noticeably elated, she gave him a broad smile and said, "That's wonderful. You have the lead."

"Yes," he replied with a tone of disappointment. "But the snake has all the lines."

Now, to those of us who have lived a few more years than that little fellow, this may seem like a rather unimportant disappointment when com-

pared to some of the disappointments we've all ago-
nized over. But for him at that time it was very real
and painful.

An early memory

My first conscious brush with what it means to be
desperately disappointed happened when I was
only three and one-half years old, but even today it
stands out vividly in my memory. My mother was
expecting a baby, and as the time for her delivery
drew near, she and my father decided that it would
be better to have me out of the way. So plans were
made for me to go to Uvalde, Texas, to stay with my
six aunts and my grandfather—grandmother was to
be in Italy, Texas, with my mother.

The timing couldn't have been better because my
Aunt Annie Merle, who was at Baylor University in
Waco, Texas, planned to take a train to Uvalde that
would pass right through Italy where we lived. Arrangements were made with the trainmaster to flag
down the afternoon train. Aunt Annie would stand
on the rear platform, and as the train slowed to a
momentary stop, my father was to hand me up to
her. It was a perfect plan, and I was caught up in a
frenzy of excitement.

The big day arrived. Daddy harnessed up the
team of horses to our buggy, and we drove along the
dusty farm road to the railroad station. It was a raw,
March day, but I was excited, and I can remember
sitting tall in the buggy adorned in my best Sunday
clothes as we rode toward town. We arrived at the

old yellow Katy station well before train time, so Daddy and I sat in the buggy while we waited. As fathers do, he gave me last minute instructions, "Now, Frances," he said, "you be a good girl and mind your aunts. Mama and Daddy want to be proud of you."

And, of course, I would agree to anything—even that. I knew those doting aunts of mine would let me do almost anything I wanted. I sat and fidgeted and listened restlessly to Daddy. Believe me, I was wound up as tight as a spring.

Finally, way off in the distance the train whistle pierced the late afternoon quiet, and as Daddy and I strained to see down the long stretch of tracks, the headlight on the old, black, steam locomotive blinked into sight. We scrambled down from the buggy and edged as close to the tracks as we could.

In a few minutes the steam engine chugged and puffed slowly by, and one by one the passenger cars moved past us. Daddy lifted me up in his arms ready to hand me up to Aunt Annie, but then, for some reason we'll never know, the train picked up just enough speed so that when the observation car moved past, there was no way Daddy could hand me up to Aunt Annie's outstretched arms. And as I watched the train and my aunt fade into the distance, I burst into tears and sobbed as only a hurt and disappointed child can cry.

Later, my mother reminded me that I cried most of the night. But by morning arrangements had been made for Daddy to take me on the next train for Uvalde. I still remember just how special I felt because I had my dad all to myself during the more than three-hundred-mile trip to Uvalde in southwest Texas. My keen disappointment and hurt were healed by my father's loving attention.

Now, these stories about two disappointed children may not seem at all tragic at the stage of life at which you and I find ourselves today. But we've all experienced the deep hurt, and, at times, bitter despair that have pressed us down so hard that we seemed to lose our ability to keep life in perspective.

The disappointments that rock our lives—the "what might have been's"—are indeed hard times . . . sometimes harder than death itself. I don't think God sends these to us, but I do believe he can provide grace that will carry us through the hard times and turn disappointments into glorious victories.

There are two examples of intense disappointment that shine through the Old Testament story which can speak vividly to us as we confront our hard times of disappointment in these waning years of the twentieth century.

The Moses saga

The first was born an undesirable alien, condemned to death even before birth simply because he was male. Moses was his name. Those were hard and bitter times for Moses' parents and for their fellow Hebrews. In their slavery they knew well the meaning of ultimate disappointment and pain. They had no civil rights, but were forced to knuckle under to the slightest whim of an autocratic and cruel king whose taskmasters constantly demanded the impossible.

The story of Moses' escape from death shortly after birth because of the cleverness of his mother Jochabed and his sister Miriam, and the drama of his boyhood and early life is a saga of adventure—all told in the early chapters of the Book of Exodus. But I want us to pick him up years later after his genius and obedience to God had combined to make him the leader of his people.

The escape from Egypt

Moses was the human instrument that moved that scraggly and rebellious horde of between two and three million Hebrews out across the Egyptian borders into the Negev and pointed toward the Promised Land across the Jordan River where once more they would be a free people. How Moses must have dreamed of being at home in his own country!

Some three months after the escape from Egypt Moses and the Israelites arrived at the base of Mount Sinai where they set up camp and spent several months. And it was here that God gave Moses the Ten Commandments inscribed on two slabs of stone.

The following spring the Israelites left their Mount Sinai camp and headed north toward the southern borders of Canaan. Upon their arrival at Kadesh Barnea weeks later, they established camp while Moses sent out twelve scouts to survey the land as a means of determining the proper strategy for the coming invasion. When the twelve scouts returned from their reconnaissance trip, ten of them gave a gloomy report. They insisted it would be impossible to conquer the walled cities of Canaan. On the other hand, two of the scouts were optimistic about their chances.

The forty-year detour

But the people of Israel were frightened by the "scouts of doom," and in spite of the word of the Lord and the pleadings of Moses, they refused to go on. And because of their disobedience God decreed that they must continue their stay in the southern wilderness and desert country until all of that generation had died. Because of fear and disobedience, that which was to have been a short trip ended up a detour of almost forty years.

It isn't hard to imagine that every day of those years in the wild and dust-laden desert—under the relentless semi-tropical sun—a fierce dream lived in Moses' breast. How often he must have said, "God, how long? I'm getting old and weary."

Moses' great disappointment

But then came the day when the wandering Hebrews moved north into the kingdom of Sihon in the land of the Amorites and camped in the plains of Moab in Trans-Jordan. And it was here that God told Moses to climb the heights of Mount Nebo where he would have a view of the land across Jordan. But it was also here that God affirmed the truth that Moses would die without ever setting foot in his Promised Land.

The Bible story doesn't describe it, but can't you just imagine the disappointment Moses felt as his forty-year dream faded away completely, like a mirage in the steaming desert? And yet it is obvious that his vigorous faith in God enabled him to conquer that disappointment, for we find no hint of it in his farewell address to the Hebrews as he gives his final blessing to them. And shortly after that he turned his steps up the slopes of Mount Nebo and climbed to its peak of some 2,600 feet to get a God-conducted preview of the homeland he'd never feel beneath his feet.

My, how good God is, though, for we read that Moses' eyesight received a heavenly touch, and he was actually able to see across the Jordan River to the walled city of Jericho with its stately palm trees. Then as he looked south, his eyes took in the vast wasteland of the Negev. To the west about 65 miles shimmered the sparkling water of the Mediterranean Sea, and way up north, more than 100 miles away near the Sidonian border and Mount Lebanon, he could see Dan. What a marvelous panorama of beauty! And as he looked, the Lord said to him, "This is the land of which I swore to Abraham, to Isaac, and to Jacob, 'I will give it to your descendants.'" Then the Lord continued, "I have let you see it with your eyes, but you shall not go over there" (Deut. 34:4, RSV).

Being human, I just have to believe that once again Moses felt the penetrating pangs of disappointment. Now he had seen the land of his dream, and yet the Lord said he couldn't go. In a way it doesn't seem fair. If I had written the script for that scene, I would have had Moses striding triumphantly across the Jordan ahead of all the Hebrews. I would have had him standing on the Canaan side of the river waving to the people as they walked past. Then I would have had Moses lead the march around the city of Jericho until the walls tumbled down on the seventh day. And immediately after that first great victory, Moses could have died. No disappointment for Moses there! He could have died in triumph—a happy and fulfilled 120-year-old man.

Moses' legacy

How's that for a happy-ever-after scenario? But our ways are not God's ways—especially in the hard times of our lives. The great lesson for us here, though, is that Moses must have handled the hard time of disappointment in a way that pleased God. For the Book of Deuteronomy closes with this magnificent tribute, "There has never been a prophet in Israel like Moses; the Lord spoke with him face-to-face. No other prophet has ever done miracles and wonders like those that the Lord sent Moses to perform against the king of Egypt, his officials and the entire country. No other prophet has been able to do the great and terrifying things that Moses did in the sight of all Israel" (Deut. 34:10–12, TEV). And in the third chapter of the book of Hebrews, when speaking of Jesus, the writer says, "He was faithful to the one who appointed him just like Moses, who stayed faithful in all his house . . ." (v. 2, JB).

And you will remember that when Jesus took Peter, James, and John up the mountain to be alone where "he was transfigured" before them, it was Moses, along with Elijah, who appeared before them and talked with Jesus (Mark 9:1–8). These and other references to Moses give me the confidence to know that he did not become bitter, despondent, and depressed when this final chapter in his life didn't work out the way he had planned. Also, it has to be clear that Moses didn't pout and get mad at God. Instead, I have to believe that his faith carried him through any momentary feeling of disappointment he probably had in his surrender to the perfect plan of God. Otherwise, I don't believe it would have been said of him that "he stayed faithful."

The David saga

There is another Old Testament hero of mine who is a classic example of a man who conquered many disappointments. His is a marvelous story! In fact, I sometimes wish we Christians could read our Bible as story. For that's what it is—God's story. Somehow, though, we have lost sight of that, and in doing so, I believe some great truths remain hidden from us. I sometimes wonder if the decorative black or brown or red covers, the thin Bible

29

paper, and the gold edges don't give us a setting where we miss the earthiness as well as the beauty and raw truth of the Bible story.

Now, don't misunderstand, I am firmly convinced that our Bible is God's inspired Word. I think the Apostle Paul was divinely inspired when he wrote, "All Scripture is God-breathed and is useful for teaching, rebuking, correcting and training in righteousness" (2 Tim. 3:16, NIV). But I don't believe this truth should cause us to lose sight of another truth—the ongoing story of how God worked in and through the lives of very human men and women is an amazing saga of adventure. Through these stories we can capture flesh and blood illustrations of God's leading and power. There is nothing old or outdated about the way they thought and acted. Human nature has remained much the same throughout the course of history. And in so many ways these stories give us insights into people that are as up-to-date as tomorrow's newspaper.

This other Old Testament hero of mine is David. His life is one grand series of climactic events. David was a doer from the early years of his life. At no time did David stoop to being a spectator in God's story; he was always a participant. But I want to zero in on one part of his story in which he was confronted with an extreme disappointment.

From the moment of King Saul's death and thirty-year-old David's succession to the throne of Israel, the new king set out to subdue their remaining enemies and complete the unification of the country. One of his first moves was to storm the heights of the Canaanite city of Jebus as a means of securing an important route to the east. Again the Lord was with him, as he had been throughout David's many battles, and Israel's armies conquered the stronghold. Jebus became Jerusalem, the City of David, and here he established his spiritual and temporal capital on the slopes of Mount Zion.

But David and his armies were not allowed to relax for long. When word reached the Philistines, Israel's traditional enemy, that David was now king, they massed their forces in a major effort to defeat David once and for all. The next movement of the story, though, tells us that the Lord outlined the battle strategy, and the Philistines were routed so completely that they were never again to be a threat during David's lifetime.

With peace firmly established, David now turned his attention to building a home—a palace—suitable for his role as king. And with the help of his friend and ally, Hiram, King of Tyre, he obtained the finest wood and materials. But when his own house was finished and David was settled in comfort, his conscience was troubled. While he rested comfortably "in a house of cedar," the ark of the Lord reposed in a simple tent. When he shared his feelings and concern with Nathan, his prophet-confidant, he was told to go ahead and fulfill the long-held dream of building a permanent temple for God.

David's disappointment

But within a few hours Nathan had fresh word from the Lord, and it was bad news for David. Because his hands were stained with the blood of many wars, David was not to be the builder of God's house: "You are not the man to build me a house to dwell in" (1 Chron. 17:4, JB) was the conclusive word. Instead, that honor would be left for Solomon, David's son and heir apparent to the throne.

Imagine David's keen disappointment! Despite the intensity of his human frailties God had been with David. His was a reign of unusual success; the nation of Israel was unified and commanded the respect of the world of that day. But now David's dream was shattered, and a peak opportunity of his career was lost.

We get a hint of how strongly he felt in a later conversation David had with his son: " 'My son,' David said to Solomon, 'my heart was set on building a house for the name of Yahweh my God'" (1 Chron. 22:7, JB). David's *heart was set* . . . it had been his dream. He wanted desperately to build this great and final expression of love for the Lord who was still his shepherd and who had led him many times "through the valley of the shadow of death." But it was not to be.

Again, we have to feel David's disappointment, for he was "every inch a man"—in both his strengths and weaknesses. There is no way I can conceive of David at this crisis moment other than as a man crushed by disappointment even though the story as we have it does not include that tragic picture.

David's legacy

But David's own words when he prayed in the next part of the story tell us how he handled any disappointment he must have felt: "Therefore thou art great, O Lord God; for there is none like thee, and there is no God besides thee, according to all that we have heard with our ears" (2 Sam. 7:22, RSV). And then as the next chapter of the story unravels, we see David, with no show of disappointment or bitterness, discussing the whole matter of the new temple with Solomon, his son, who someday would supervise the building.

Living models

These two great patriarchs of our faith offer us living models of how to respond to the hard times of disappointment which are a part of our daily experience. It is clear from these two stories that both Moses and David had infinite trust in God. At the same time their stories also reveal the intensity of their humanness. They fell short of the glory of God and frequently "missed the mark." And yet they had discovered that the purposes of God may be hard at times for us to understand. But they had a living awareness in their hard times of disappointment of a truth well expressed later by the prophet Isaiah when he wrote, "For my thoughts are not your thoughts, neither are your ways my ways, says the Lord. For as the heavens are higher than the earth, so are my ways higher than your ways and my thoughts than your thoughts" (Isa. 55:8–9, RSV).

But I know so well that even with models like Moses and David and reassurance like these words from Isaiah, it is easy for us in the rush of life to let disappointments either defeat us or send us on a course that is second best. When we confront feelings of disappointment with ourselves because we acted or reacted badly . . . or when we have been disappointed with a husband or a wife or with our children . . . or when we've experienced feelings of disappointment with our friends—it is so easy to berate and put ourselves down by dwelling on a series of "what ifs."

The "if only" syndrome

Robert Raines captured this idea so clearly when he wrote, "But so often we're blind and deaf to God's presence in our difficulties because of our own pain or anger, resentment, self-pity. We indulge in what may be called the 'if only' syndrome. If only I had another job, if only my boss would move or have a heart attack, if only I could make another five or ten thousand a year. If only I weren't short and pimply-faced, or tall and awkward, or successful and empty. If only my parents would listen to me. If only my kids would do what I tell them. If only I didn't have allergy, nervous colon, omnipresent in-laws, a house decaying under my feet and teeth decaying in my mouth. If only, if only, if only. Growth begins when we stop saying 'if only' and start to recognize that difficulties are opportunities to grow."[1]

The choice is ours. Hard times of disappointment can turn us into unpleasant and defeated people or lead us to the place of spiritual growth and victory.

With keen insight Eleanor Roosevelt once said, "Our philosophy is best expressed, not in words, but in the choices one makes in daily living."

We decide the results

Our challenge as Christians—as children of the all-powerful and ever-loving God—when tempted to stoop low under what we believe to be a burden of disappointments, is to claim the words of the prophet when he said, "Should you pass through the sea, I will be with you; or through the rivers, they will not swallow you up. Should you walk through fire, you will not be scorched and the flames will not burn you" (Isa. 43:2, JB).

With that confidence we can then begin to understand even just a little bit of what Frederick Faber meant when he said, "There are no disappointments to those whose wills are buried in the will of God."

When Roy and I were married, we both agreed that we would like a large family of children. We dreamed long life for each of them as they gave themselves to the Lord. By God's grace we have tried to set a good example for our children, and this is not to say that we haven't stumbled ourselves from time to time. However, the intent of our hearts has been to obey God's Word as best we understood it. We dreamed of raising all of our children—our natural ones and our adopted ones—never once considering the possibility of loss by death. We adopted children that we felt had a special need, and we had the joy of seeing them flower for a time before death took two of them by accident and our baby by illness. At each of those moments we could have bowed our heads and shouted, "Why?" But instead we chose to trust God even in our moments of anger and deep hurt. We've had to learn to pray, "Not my will but thine be done."

For the Christian, disappointments are opportunities to learn more of Christ and of his will for our lives. And it is in our disappointments that we learn to live out the words, "And we know that in all things God works for the good of those who love him . . ." (Rom. 8:28, NIV).

God in the Hard Times
of Loneliness   3.

_____

*". . . there is another healer for this
hard time in our lives—we can be
sensitive to the needs of those around us
and offer ourselves and our services to
people who are sorely in need of a
friend. And in spite of the facades that
people wear, there is an almost
universal longing on their part for
someone to listen to them, to talk with
them, and share in their hurts and
anxieties. Our loneliness, when
harnessed to helpfulness, can be a
tremendous blessing to someone else."*

"Be strong and courageous; have no fear . . . for it is the Lord your God that is going with you; he will neither fail you nor forsake you."

Deuteronomy 31:6, MLB

_____

"LIFE IS A TALE told by an idiot, full of sound and fury, signifying nothing."

Seldom has cynicism found more poignant expression than in the words Shakespeare planted on Macbeth's lips. Yet these words echo the hopelessness so often felt and expressed when we are wrestling with the hard times of loneliness and discouragement and rejection in our lives.

It isn't likely that any of us—you or me—would describe our lives as "tales told by an idiot," but most of us have vivid memories of times when we've felt terribly alone and rejected. Dr. Viktor Frankl, the prominent Viennese psychiatrist who survived the German extermination camps during the Second World War, has said that loneliness and feelings of alienation and rejection are a universal illness of our time. And Thomas Wolfe, a gifted novelist, admitted that "loneliness, far from being a rare and curious phenomenon, peculiar to myself and to a few other solitary men, is the central and inevitable fact of human existence."

Lonely but not alone

Believe me, there have been times in my life when I felt desperately alone and rejected and discouraged. More than fifty years have passed, but I remember well the crushing loneliness and bitter feelings of rejection when my first husband walked out on me—a sixteen-year-old mother of a baby son. In my outrageous immaturity and crippling insecurity, I lashed out at anyone within striking distance and built up a high, protective wall around myself, vowing never to be hurt that way again.

Finally, after four or five years of struggling as a secretary, as a radio singer in Memphis, and then as a fifteen-dollar-a-week secretary in Chicago—still mad at the world and feeling more lonely and rejected than ever before in my life—I gave up and accepted an invitation from my mother and father to "come home." And there, in that little central Texas town of Italy, I found healing for myself and love and security for my little son Tommy. I'll never forget, either, the unqualified acceptance Mother and Dad gave me. Yes, they hadn't approved of most of what had happened in my life to that point, but in their love they accepted me just as I was. And because of that I regained courage and hope and was soon out again pursuing my career.

Elijah—God's chosen man

How like God Mother and Dad were during those days! They exemplified in so many ways a marvelous story in the Old Testament about the patience and love of God. I'm referring to a most interesting chapter in the life of one of God's special prophets—Elijah. In fact, Elijah was so special to God that he had a privileged spot, along with Moses, on the Mount of Transfiguration when they both visited with Jesus.

Elijah first appears on the scene in the seventeenth chapter of First Kings. He then occupies center stage in Israel through several more chapters until his miraculous "translation," as told in the second chapter of Second Kings. What a story!

Elijah was a gutsy man. I like to think he would have felt very much at home in some of the western movies Roy and I did at Republic Studios. Elijah was a man of passion, of deep feelings. When he was on an emotional high, he was very high. And when he was low, look out! But we can't venture far in Elijah's story without realizing that God was with him in a special way.

Now, one of Elijah's first tasks as God's prophet was unpleasant—he was the messenger of bad news. He told Ahab, king of Israel, that there was going to be a drought and famine that would dry up the land and make it barren and useless. And it all happened just like Elijah said.

But in the midst of the incredibly bad conditions that crippled Israel, God personally looked out for Elijah by telling him to go live by a creek or brook called Cherith that ran close by his home town of Tishbeh, about twenty-two miles south of the Sea of Chinnereth, later known as the Sea of Galilee. Cherith flowed west into the River Jordan. There, according to the story, Elijah was miraculously fed bread and meat twice a day, and he drew fresh drinking water from Cherith.

Everything went fine until the brook dried up. But then the word of the Lord came to Elijah, and he was instructed to break camp and travel north and west almost eighty miles to the town of Zarephath on the Mediterranean coast in Phoenicia, just a few miles south of Sidon in what is Lebanon today. There he is fed and cared for by a widow whose larder God keeps full even though famine and suffering exist all around them. And it is there, too, that Elijah performs one of the five miracles credited to his ministry when through fervent prayer he brings the widow's dead son back to life.

I recall so well my visit several years ago to this very region of Tyre and Sidon. What a thrill it was to walk in the ancient footsteps of Elijah and Jesus. My mind and heart both raced as I recalled Jesus' visit to the home of the Greek woman whose daughter was mentally ill—possessed with a demon. But because of the mother's faith and persistence, Jesus healed the little girl completely. Truly, this was for me a sacred place as I remembered the stories of both Jesus and Elijah.

The prophet's test

But back to our Elijah story. Finally, after three and one-half years of intense heat and drought, God tells Elijah that soon rain will once again fall on Israel. But before that happens we are treated to one of those rare scenes that is both tragic and humorous but which ends in a great affirmation of God's power.

In 1 Kings 18 we read about the amazing contest between the four hundred and fifty prophets of Baal and Elijah, the prophet of God, on the slopes of Mount Carmel. This was precipitated by the challenge Elijah gave all the Israelites gathered on the mountain when he said, "How long will you go limping with two opinions? If the Lord is God, follow him; but if Baal, follow him." As the story unravels to this point, we find that none of the Israelites was ready to make a decision.

So, at Elijah's suggestion, the four hundred and fifty prophets of Baal built an altar, stacked it high with dry wood, laid a bull sacrifice on top, and called upon their god to send down fire to burn the sacrifice. From early morning until high noon the prophets of Baal pleaded with their god to send fire, but nothing happened. With rare humor Elijah taunted them by suggesting that maybe Baal had fallen asleep and possibly it would help if they made more noise and hollered louder. This they did, but still there came no answer and no fire.

Now it was Elijah's turn. He carefully repaired the altar of the Lord that had stood for so long on Mount Carmel. Then he stacked wood on it and laid a bull sacrifice on top of the wood. Next he doused the wood and the sacrifice with water until it was heavily soaked.

Elijah was playing a dangerous game, but he knew his God. Standing before the altar with water running from it into a ditch that surrounded it, he prayed, and "the fire of the Lord fell, and consumed the burnt offering, and the wood, and the stones, and the dust and licked up the water that was in the trench." Wow! God didn't do it half way—even the stones and the dust were incinerated and the water evaporated into thin air. Elijah had proved his point with God's help, and the people were convinced that "the Lord, he is God; the Lord, he is God." And with that, they killed all of the false prophets of the pagan god Baal.

The contract on Elijah's life

But now the scene shifts back to King Ahab's palace. When he tells his wife Jezebel all that has happened, she is furious, and in a fit of murderous anger she sends word to Elijah that within twenty-four hours she's going to see him dead—she put out a contract on his life.

I'm sure you've heard it said that there is no fury like that of a woman scorned—and Jezebel was scorned! Elijah had trampled on all she held dear by outsmarting, with God's help, her prophets of Baal.

She felt personally humiliated and repudiated. Maybe Ahab would take this without a fight, but not Jezebel!

Then the story takes an odd twist. Elijah had stood fearlessly against four hundred and fifty of the enemy. With a boldness characteristic of this rugged man of God, he had defied a mighty and autocratic king. But when Jezebel laid her curse on him, he became frightened, turned the other way, and ran for his life. We read that he scurried south to Beersheba, left his servant-companion there, and ran another day's journey into the desolate wilderness of the Negev. When he felt safe and was certain that no one had followed him, Elijah sat down under a juniper tree and asked God to let him die: "O Lord, take away my life; for I am no better than my fathers."

Imagine! Here was the man that God had fed at Cherith . . . at Zarephath God had miraculously kept food in the widow's pantry, and it was here, too, that God enabled Elijah to give life back to a dead boy . . . on Mount Carmel Elijah was God's instrument to bring down fire on the water-soaked altar. Over the years Elijah had seen the mighty and holy God of the Israelites in control of all his creation. Never once had God failed Elijah.

Elijah's despair and a gentle God

But suddenly, all of this seemed to be forgotten . . . it was as if Elijah's blood had turned to water, and he was deathly afraid. In fact, he seemed

45

to forget all of the glorious victories God had given him. Now he was afraid and depressed, alone in the wilderness of his confused mind with only the wild and parched Negev for his home. Now there seemed only one way out of his despair, "O Lord, take away my life."

If I had been God, Elijah would have gotten a good-sized piece of my mind right then. I would have been completely out of patience with him and would have written him off as being undependable and ungrateful—a wretched coward that couldn't be trusted with the future.

But God understood Elijah in his fear and aloneness and discouragement. He didn't add to Elijah's feelings of rejection with a reprimand as so many of us would probably have done. Instead, twice God sent an angel into that wild and desolate spot to feed Elijah and to give him life-sustaining water. And after a time, God told Elijah to move on to Mount Horeb where he was directed to a cave which was to be his home for a while.

Evidently, though, Elijah was still wrapped tightly in his feelings of loneliness and rejection. He was still feeling sorry for himself, for when God came to the cave and asked how he was doing, in so many words Elijah said that *everyone* else had deserted him . . . he alone was faithful to the Lord. Elijah was evidently traumatized by crippling depression—a debilitating mood brought on because of his feelings of loneliness and rejection.

But once more God was gentle and patient with

Elijah, for again, on the rugged slopes of Horeb God paraded his awesome might and power in front of Elijah. And out of the stillness of a dramatic moment of silence the Lord spoke and the prophet heard. Reassurance came that Elijah was not alone—there were others faithful to Israel's God. The time was past when the prophet could bask in the misery of his loneliness and discouragement. His marching orders were to move out from the wilderness of despair and get back into action.

What an incredible lesson there is for us in the Elijah story! In our littleness and near-sighted vision we sometimes get the idea that we are alone . . . that the forces of the enemy of our souls are winning all the battles . . . that there is no one but us in the economy of God who sees things quite right . . . our interpretation is the only right one and that all others are wrong. Then when things don't move along in God's kingdom just the way we think they should, we feel rejected and persecuted and discouraged and alone. At such moments feelings of defeat smother the impact of earlier victories, and we become useless to God and everyone else. Then, like Elijah, we sit down under our own particular juniper tree, broken and discouraged. We have become so immersed in our own ideas, so intent on our privileges, and so dogmatically certain of our interpretation of the law and the gospel that we have actually become blind to the greatness and majesty and love of God. And it is at such moments that we are most vulnerable to Satan's attack.

Jesus stands alone

By contrast, much later in our biblical story we read of Another. Jesus had moved up and down Palestine healing broken lives and witnessing to the power of God. The crowds had virtually mobbed him at times because of their enthusiasm for him and his words. But on the night of his arrest, after having been betrayed by one from his intimate circle of friends, we read that "all the disciples deserted him and ran away."

Jesus was alone, rejected by the crowds and by his closest friends. There was no one to stand with him in the inner sanctum of the high priest's palace. Never was a man more alone! These were moments designed for bitterness in the midst of what appeared to be crushing defeat.

But there was none of Elijah's paranoia in Jesus' words and actions. Instead, he responded to his tormentors' trickery by defining his identity in a few calm words, ". . . you will see the Son of man seated at the right hand of power coming on the clouds of heaven." He knew who he was and no accent of discouragement or rejection could be found in his words.

And then, as if that isn't enough, a little later, Luke, perhaps the most precise storyteller of the Gospel writers, focuses on one of the more poignant scenes found in our Bible. The setting is an intimate one—in the courtyard of the high priest's house: "They had lit a fire in the middle of the courtyard and Peter sat down among them, and as he was sitting there by the blaze a servant girl saw him, peered at him, and said, 'This person was with him too.' But he denied it. 'Woman,' he said, 'I do not know him.' Shortly afterward someone else saw him and said, 'You are one of them.' But Peter replied, 'I am not, my friend.' About an hour later another man insisted, saying, 'This fellow was certainly with him. Why, he is a Galilean.' 'My friend,' said Peter, 'I do not know what you are talking about'" (Luke 22:55–60, JB).

Just a few hours earlier this same Peter had said to Jesus, "I would be ready to go to prison with you, and to death." Now, under the stress of the moment, he says three times that he doesn't even know him.

If ever a person had the right to feel deserted and rejected, it was Jesus at that dark moment. How his humanity must have felt outraged! But, let's go back to Luke's telling of the story, "At that instant, while he was still speaking, the cock crew, and *the Lord turned and looked straight at Peter*, and Peter remembered what the Lord had said to him, 'Before the cock crows today, you will have disowned me three times'" (Luke 22:61–62, JB, italics mine).

A victor not a victim

We hear no words of rebuke or bitterness from Jesus. There's no smell of paranoia here, no depression, and no tone of discouragement . . . just a look, and knowing my Lord, I have to believe it was a look of compassion—a look of patient understanding. And how thoughtful our Lord was under these circumstances, for later, on the glorious Resurrection morning, Luke reports: ". . . and they found the eleven gathered together and those who were with them, who said, 'The Lord has risen indeed, and has appeared to Simon [Peter].'"

The Apostle Paul validates this sequence of the story, ". . . he was raised on the third day in accordance with the scriptures, and that he appeared to Cephas [Peter], then to the twelve. Then he appeared to more than five hundred brethren at one time . . ." (1 Cor. 15:4–6, RSV). According to Luke, Peter was one of the first, if not *the* first, of Jesus' intimate friends to see the Lord after his victory over death and the grave. What a wonderful Lord we have, and he models for us the ultimate response to our very human feelings of loneliness and rejection and discouragement.

Centuries before, the Psalmist, with rare intuitive insight, gave us a powerful word for those moments when we feel tempted to think that everything has gone wrong, that we are deserted and rejected, that we are alone: "God is our refuge and strength, a very present help in trouble. Therefore we will not fear though the earth should change, though the mountains shake in the heart of the sea; though its waters roar and foam, though the mountains tremble with its tumult" (Ps. 46:1–3, RSV).

An epidemic of loneliness

But I know from my travels back and forth across the country and from talking with thousands of people that an epidemic of loneliness is creeping through our way of life. We lose touch with our family, with our neighbors, and even with each other in our churches. Everyone seems so caught up in the rush of life that we forget the promises like the one found in the forty-sixth Psalm. Richard Foster describes our condition this way, "In contemporary society our Adversary majors in three things: noise, hurry, and crowds. If he can keep us engaged in 'muchness' and 'manyness,' he will rest satisfied."[1] Then, there's a marvelous comment attributed to Dr. C. G. Jung that speaks to the hurry of our time, "Hurry is not *of* the Devil; it *is* the Devil."

Most certainly, it is hurry and noise and crowds that cut us off from each other so that we feel terribly alone, even in a crowd. Indeed, our Western culture, with its burgeoning urban centers, laced by dehumanizing freeways with cars darting in and out and around in a frantic rush to get somewhere, has become a breeding ground for loneliness. Then, too, there's an emptiness and an emotional poverty in the midst of our affluence, and we feel horribly alone and cut off and disconnected from others even in this time of spellbinding communication know-how. So often we're unable to talk with each other and yet we can hear the voices of our astronauts from hundreds of miles out in space, and we're able to receive signals from space craft moving out of our solar system.

In one way or another this affects us all. In a moment of deep hurt, the late Judy Garland said, "If I'm a legend, then why am I so lonely?" But again I say, such moments of doubt and questioning are not confined to people in show business. We all have our moments of feeling isolated and alone, and we rub shoulders with people every day whose faces betray unrest and confusion—especially in their "hard times" moments.

A very discouraged and confused young man told his landlady one day that he was all through trying and was going down to the river to commit suicide. Because of the obvious depth of his depression she knew this wasn't an idle threat, so she tried desperately to talk him out of it. Finally, he said, "If I meet just one person between here and the river who gives me a word of encouragement or a smile, it would make life worth living, and I'll come back." He didn't; she never saw him alive again.

Alone, discouraged, and depressed—this young man gave up because he was without hope. Dr. Eugene Kennedy expressed well the paradox of our times when he wrote, "The American landscape is filled with the evidence of man's loneliness and with his attempts to cope in some way or another with it. It is streaked with paradox, men feeling alone in the midst of a population explosion; men feeling empty inside in the midst of affluence; men feeling cut off in the age of communication."[2]

Yes, in varying degrees we all experience our hard times of loneliness and of discouragement. So often we find ourselves unwittingly seduced by the negative mood of our times—and like Elijah feel that all has failed and there is no one to stand with us . . . there isn't one person along our way to give us a

smile or a word of encouragement in our hard times
that will make life worth living.

Moses points the way

But it is in such moments that we find powerful
affirmations from the Word of God. One of these is
found in the early chapters of Exodus. The people of
Israel were perched on the banks of the Red Sea.
After years of slavery and humiliating oppression,
freedom was within their grasp—the Egyptian Pharaoh had turned them loose and agreed to let them
leave the country. But as they faced the formidable
obstacle of the impassable body of water, word
reached them that Pharaoh regretted his decision
and had sent his army to bring them back into
slavery.

There they stood—more than a million milling
and undisciplined people—at the water's edge.
They couldn't go forward, and the enemy was behind them. They were alone, seemingly deserted . . . fear gave way to terror . . . terror moved
them into the intensity of mass depression. Hope
was gone, and they turned on their leader, Moses,
and said, "What have you done to us, in bringing us
out of Egypt? Is not this what we said to you in
Egypt, 'Let us alone and let us serve the Egyptians'?
For it would have been better for us to serve the
Egyptians than to die in the wilderness."

But listen now to Moses' answer, "Fear not, stand
firm, and see the salvation of the Lord, which he will

work for you today . . . the Lord will fight for you, and you have only to be still" (Exod. 14:10–18, RSV).

These same words echo down across the centuries of time and bring us encouragement in our hard times—even now in the 1980s. It is not God's will that we, at any time, succumb to the paralysis of loneliness and discouragement. Rather, it is his will that we *stand still*, *stand firm*, and see God work in our lives and in the lives of those around us.

The recipe for confidence

God gives us a forceful word through the lips of the prophet Isaiah, "Fear not, for I have redeemed you; I have called you by name, you are mine. When you pass through the waters I will be with you; and through the rivers, they shall not overwhelm you . . . for I am the Lord your God" (Isa. 43:1–3, RSV).

What a breathtaking promise: *I have redeemed you; I have called you by name, you are mine!* The Lord assures us that we are his, and the word of the Lord here gives us positive assurance that we are never alone. There is just no room for feelings of loneliness. But at the same time we have no assurance from the Lord that he will keep us from having hard times or will provide answers before our moment of real need.

We *can* be certain, though, that as we stand on the raw edge of our need, God will meet us—even as he met the needs of the people of Israel when he performed a miracle and opened up a path for them *through* the sea and saved them from what appeared to be sure doom.

I recall so well in 1948, after I had committed my life to Jesus Christ, there were times when I felt a crushing sense of loneliness among my peers in show business. They thought I had gone "off the deep end" in my Christian experience and lifestyle. One day an actress friend asked, "Evans, what is the matter with you? You are not the same . . ."

And I wasn't the same. Instead of "Evans" being on the throne of my life, Jesus was. This meant that I was no longer interested in some of the worldly activities that had filled my life before. Let me tell you, I felt very alone and lonely even in the midst of the people and the busyness in my professional life.

Then, too, I had many lonely moments at home because it wasn't until several weeks after my own experience that Roy entered into a relationship with God through Jesus Christ. During those lonely days and nights the Adversary would sneak up on me and say, "Keep your faith to yourself. You are turning people off. They don't want you around to be a wet blanket." Those were desperate days for me, but again and again I received comfort and peace from such promises as found in Hebrews 13:5, "God himself has said: *I will not fail you or desert you . . .*" (JB).

Lessons learned

Indeed, the Word of God with its many promises can be our haven during the hard times of loneliness. The words of assurance as found in Psalm 27:10 have frequently been a source of strength to me: "When my father and my mother forsake me, then the Lord will take me up" (KJV). In other words, even when those who are the closest to us "leave" us for any reason, God will "gather us up" to himself and give us the lift we need to overcome our feelings of loneliness.

But there is another healer for this hard time in our lives—we can be sensitive to the feelings of those around us and offer ourselves and our services to people who are sorely in need of a friend. And in spite of the facades that people wear, there is an almost universal longing on their part for someone to listen to them, to talk with them, and share in their hurts and anxieties. Our loneliness, when harnessed to helpfulness, can be a tremendous blessing to someone else. It has been said, "When grief is used to bless someone else who is in the throes of loss and despair, it loses its sting for you and brings blessing not only to the other person but to you as well."

Loneliness can be a wondrous blessing when it drives us to the Master who gave us this eternal promise, "And know that I am with you always; yes, to the end of time" (Matt. 28:20, JB).

God in the Hard Times of Failure 4.

*" 'I am come that they might have life,
and that they might have it more
abundantly.' " There's no room for half-
hearted mediocrity in these words.
Rather, they are powerful words of
assurance that give us the courage to
move through life with zest and
boldness—willing to risk even the
possibility of failure, but always
knowing that 'if God be for us, who can
be against us?' "*

"There is nothing I cannot master with the help of the One who gives me strength."

Philippians 4:13, JB

IN 1915 AT THE age of forty-one, Winston Churchill confided to a friend, "I'm finished. I'm banished from the scene of action."

Just a year before, at the outbreak of the First World War, Churchill had been considered one of the most powerful and popular men in the British Empire. But a series of tragic reversals in the progress of the war drove him from his post as First Lord of the Admiralty and ultimately he was dismissed from the Cabinet—an inglorious failure at mid-life.

Early failures

I can identify easily with what Winston Churchill must have felt at that low point of failure. My own life was battered early with my failures at marriage. At a young age I tried my hand at writing short stories and suffered the humiliation of endless rejection slips. Then my first attempts at song writing ended up in the wastebasket. My later dreams of starring in a Hollywood musical comedy never materialized. I came close once, though. One day, out of the blue, I got a call from my agent Danny Winkler, "Dale, RKO Studios wants you for the ingenue lead in *Show Business Out West.*" It was to be a musical comedy starring Eddie Cantor and Joan Davis. Believe me, I was flying high, but after waiting impatiently for another call, I got the word that the picture had been scrapped.

Then years later when I wrote *Angel Unaware,* after our little Robin's death, I felt a crushing sense of failure when two publishers in a row turned it down. I didn't know at the time that I was participating in a drama with such literary greats as Margaret Mitchell, whose classic Civil War novel, *Gone with the Wind,* had been turned down by several publishers before it finally appeared in print and sold a million and a half copies in its first year.

But by this time in my life I was beginning to learn a little more about how God can work in our moments of failure, so I just turned my *Angel Unaware* manuscript over to him. On the very day I did that I received a telephone call, "Mrs. Rogers, I'm Frank

Mead from the Fleming H. Revell Company. I've heard about your manuscript and would like to read it." I rushed a copy over to him in record time, and after a few days I received a call from Dr. Mead saying that Revell wanted to publish it. They did, and, thanks be to God, that little book went out to bless thousands upon thousands of readers.

The first failure

Hard times of failure have stained the lives of men and women since the beginning of time. It all began with Adam and Eve's colossal failure—disobeying God in the Garden of Eden. Disobedience and failure thwarted God's purpose in their lives because they chose to believe a lie. Earlier God had said they could eat from all of the trees but one, ". . . of the tree of the knowledge of good and evil you are not to eat, for on the day you eat of it you shall most surely die" (Gen. 2:17, JB).

But one fateful day Adam and Eve made a calculated decision to believe the serpent when he said, " 'No! You will not die! God knows in fact that on the day you eat it your eyes will be opened and you will be like gods . . .' " (Gen. 3:5, JB). That was the beginning, and one way or another, our failures, even today, are rooted consciously or unconsciously in failure to believe and trust God.

Samson's dark days

One of the saddest, most confusing, and complex characters in our Bible drama is Samson. He appeared on the scene during some of Israel's darkest days—days described vividly as times when "every man did as he pleased."

Samson's birth was a miracle, foretold by an angel of the Lord. His parents were godly folks, who in obedience to the Lord vowed to raise him in the holy tradition of God's Nazarite—even as was John the Baptist many centuries later. He was singled out to be a special man—never to drink wine or strong drink, never to eat anything unclean, and never to shave or have his hair cut. In other words, he was to look and act differently from anyone else in Israel.

Then, according to the story, the boy grew and "the Lord blessed him" and the Spirit of the Lord "began to stir him." But next, the story takes a tragic turn. Apparently young Samson began to hobnob with the neighboring Philistines—a nation of people who had migrated from Crete and settled in what is now known as the Gaza Strip. They were a sophisticated and pagan civilization who were great admirers of physical prowess, and Samson was popular with them in spite of his intemperate use of the Herculean strength God had blessed him with.

It was only a matter of time until Samson was attracted to the sensual quality of the uninhibited Philistine women, and contrary to his father's wishes, he deserted his own people and married a pagan Philistine girl. In his poem about Samson, Milton pretty well reveals Samson's attitude when he has him boast, "Like a petty god I walked about, admired by all." That sounds a little bit like the serpent in the Garden of Eden, doesn't it?

Samson had sold out completely to the sophisticated and pagan ways of the Philistines. Even after the miserable end to his first marriage, we know he hadn't learned his lesson because we read that he married Delilah, another Philistine woman. And while all of this is going on, he continued to exploit his divinely-given strength by wreaking carnage and murder on his enemies. Completely forgotten were his Nazarite vows and the One who was the real source of his strength.

Next comes Delilah's cunning attempts to learn the secret of Samson's awesome strength. Her loyalty was not to the foreign husband she had seduced but to the Philistine authorities whose admiration of the strong man had now turned to hatred and vengeance. And after three attempts she coaxed the truth from Samson—his strength was in his long hair.

The scene now shifts to her bedroom. Here, while Samson dozed in what was probably a drunken sleep, his head was shaved. Betrayed and unable to overcome his enemies, he was bound and taken captive, his eyes were gouged out, and he was condemned to slavery. His failure is complete—what "might have been" becomes a fading fantasy.

The final act of Samson's life takes place as he is put on display one day in the temple of the pagan god Dagon. Samson is on exhibition, chained to two of the temple's main support pillars. By now his hair has grown long enough that he knows his strength has returned. With one final effort he hunches his broad back, knots his mighty muscles, and with a gigantic heave Samson pulls down the main supports of Dagon's temple. Not only was he crushed in the thunderous collapse of the building, but the story says that in that moment he killed more people than he had in all his lifetime.

Mischief, deception, lust, vengeance, murder, and self-murder are the benchmarks of Samson's career. What a sad failure for the man who had been destined to lead God's chosen people. And instead of being God's witness to the pagan Philistines he had kept building failure upon failure until in this final act of violence Samson so intensified their hatred of Israel that there was almost constant warfare until David neutralized them many years later.

I know from personal experience that the patient and tender hand of a loving God had been reaching out to Samson at each point in his life. That's just the way God is. I'm reminded so often of that scene in the New Testament in which Peter stepped out of the boat and walked on the water toward Jesus. All went well until Peter took his eyes off Jesus and looked down at the water lapping at his feet—then he started to sink. It was a moment of failure, but when he cried out to his Lord to save him, Jesus took him by the hand and lifted him up to safety. Happily, Peter knew the source of his strength even in the midst of that moment of failure.

The Moses story

But this account of how we are to respond to the hard times of failure in our lives would not be complete without another quick look into the Bible story. Long before Samson's time there was a young Hebrew who by the plan of God became a prince in Pharaoh's court in Egypt, while at the same time his countrymen were slaves of the Egyptians. As the adopted grandson of the mighty king, Moses was reared in princely grandeur. All of the advantages of that great nation were his. He was accustomed to having success and authority—a young man of action because he knew who he was. And one day he saw one of his Israelite countrymen being abused by an Egyptian. In a fit of self-righteous anger Moses took matters into his own hands and killed the Egyptian. A few hours after the murder when Moses discovered that a witness had observed his infamous act, his status changed immediately from prince to fugitive. He fled the borders of Egypt and hid out in the desert country of Midian.

The Bible story doesn't give us any details of Moses' feelings, but it isn't hard to imagine his sense of failure. After all, he had been schooled by Egypt's finest. He was doubtlessly well-educated in the arts and sciences of his time. He had a good future. Now, because of his impetuous act of violence everything he had prepared for disappeared like a mirage in the desert.

We know little of Moses' thoughts and actions at that time except that he joined forces with Jethro, married one of his daughters, and became the overseer of his father-in-law's flocks. He had been catapulted from prince to nomad-shepherd because of his moment of failure.

There is no direct hint of Moses' life during the some forty years that he lived in seclusion tending Jethro's flocks and herds in the southern wilderness, but Roy and I know from our own experience of living on the edge of the desert near Victorville, California, just how much wild and rugged and quiet desert country helps when it comes to thinking and reflecting and praying. It is a marvelous antidote to the frantic hustle and bustle of city life today.

Anyway, it isn't far-fetched to believe that Moses did a lot of thinking during those years as he moved his sheep and herds back and forth across the quiet desert. And thinking leads to *seeing* and to *listening* and to *feeling*—seeing the awesome wonders of God so visible in the vast outdoors, day and night; listening to the rhythm of nature's sounds and the breath of the Lord as the wind rustles through the desert brush; and feeling the presence of God in the warm sun, in the towering mountains, in the hollow of the heavens ablaze with countless stars, and in the silence of the unending stretches of rolling desert.

But let's pick up on the story. One day Moses, alert to the safety and well-being of his flocks, had moved them along to grazing land at the foot of Mount Horeb, "the mountain of God." And it is there, as his eyes scanned the horizon, that he saw something out of the ordinary off in the distance—a bush appeared to be on fire but was not being consumed. The bushes all around him were ordinary bushes, the floor of the valley was unchanged. It would have been so easy for a less sensitive and less observant person to have moved on along, believing that his eyes were just playing tricks on him. But Moses felt compelled to move in for a closer look. And as he did so, he heard the voice of God and the electric announcement that he had been commissioned to lead his countrymen out of Egypt's bondage and slavery.

Moses heard the voice of God. There was no princely arrogance now in his response. No longer did he believe the lie that he could take matters into his own hands—that the end justifies the means. His immediate question, "Who am I that I should go . . . ?" gives positive proof that instead of being eternally defeated by his failure of forty years ago, he had used that failure to grow and to learn and to listen to God.

Moses and Samson give us a stark contrast on handling failure. Samson never learned from his failures. In a thirst for power and identity he blundered by leaving behind the wreckage of hurt and bruised people until his only answer was death of soul and body. But in Moses we have a superb model of a doer, a man of action, whose failure at the prime of his life was used redemptively to prepare himself for a godly and useful life.

In many ways I see a strong similarity between the lives of Moses and Winston Churchill. From the low point of his failure in 1915 when Churchill issued his "I'm finished" statement, he began to rebuild. With pugnacity he held on to his dreams until with brilliant achievement he led his nation to resistance and victory in the Second World War some twenty-five years later. It was his "blood, sweat, and tears" statement at that time which ignited the imagination of millions across the world and stiffened their resistance to an evil and blood-thirsty German oppressor.

And from the low point of Moses' failure he went through forty years of behind-the-scenes preparation for the day in which he would fire the imagination of defeated slaves and lead them out of their bondage. Then, when they faced their first major crisis on the shores of the Red Sea and were ready to give up, Moses made his Churchillian statement, "Fear not, stand firm, and see the salvation of the Lord, which he will work for you today" (Exod. 14:13, RSV).

Attitude makes a difference

How often in my terribly human and action-filled lifetime have I leaned heavily on those words of Moses, "Fear not, stand firm, and see the salvation of the Lord." Let's face it, we all fail. Dr. Phillips expressed it so well in his translation of Romans 3:23, "Everyone has sinned, everyone falls short of the beauty of God's plan." Yes, because of our impetuous actions we can expect to have our hard times of failure, but it is our attitude in those moments that makes the difference.

This truth is graphically illustrated by the life of Abraham Lincoln, the sixteenth president of the United States. In 1832 he was defeated as a candidate for the Illinois legislature. Not long after, he failed in business. In 1834 he won a seat in the Illinois legislature and was reelected in 1836, 1838, and 1840. But sometime between 1840 and 1842 he became so depressed that he contemplated suicide. In 1846 he was elected to the United States Congress but failed to be renominated in 1848. Then in 1854 he was elected to the Illinois legislature against his will, but later resigned to run for the United States Senate and was defeated. In 1858 he ran for the Senate again and suffered defeat. And finally, in 1860 he won the nomination for the presidency by the Republican party and was elected but with a minority of popular vote. From there, Abraham Lincoln went on to lead the United States through the troubled and tragic years of the Civil War and to the peace that assured an end of slavery and brought healing to the divided nation.

Few men are as revered in American history as Lincoln. And the secret rests, I believe, in his attitude toward failure. Without recrimination he moved from his failures to success and victory. It was his spirit and dependency upon God that made the difference. And for us, there is one sure formula that when followed can turn our failures into victory. It is found in Paul's words to the Philippians, "There is nothing I cannot master with the help of the One who gives me strength" (Phil. 4:13, JB). What a powerful affirmation of faith that is! I'll guarantee that any person who makes a habit of repeating those powerful words several times daily, week in and week out, will have a life-changing experience of growth in faith—the kind of faith Martin

Luther describes as a "living, daring confidence in God's grace. It is so sure and certain that a man could stake his life on it a thousand times."

The case of total failure

But there are other failures that we don't think much about because they do not make headlines in block letters. In fact, we tend to gloss them over and not even think of them as failures. This is illuminated graphically by Jesus, one of the greatest storytellers who ever lived. The story was about a rather affluent man who had three servants working for him. Jesus said that this man was getting ready to go off on a trip, but before leaving he called in the three servants and gave one of them five talents. To the second man he gave two talents, and to the third man he gave one talent.

The first man took his five talents and invested them; the man with the two talents did the same thing. But the third man took his one talent and buried it in the ground for safekeeping.

After quite a long time the employer returned from his trip and called the three servants in for an accounting of the talents he had entrusted to them.

The first man brought in the original five talents plus the five more he had earned through wise investment. He was commended highly by his master and well rewarded for his good judgment. The second man brought in the two talents that had been given him plus two more, and he was complimented and rewarded. Both of these men had doubled the value of that which had been given to them. But the third man went out and dug up the buried talent that had been given him and brought it in. His master was very upset with him for not putting to good use what had been entrusted to him and castigated him severely for his lack of stewardship. And as a penalty for his bad judgment, the talent was taken away from him, and he was thrown out—the final loser; the total failure.

The failure of mediocrity

Without taking undue liberties, the word "gifts" can properly be substituted for "talents" in this story. God has given all of us special gifts—gifts that can enrich our own lives and the lives of others around us. But so often, because of a fear of failure, we are not willing to take the necessary risks to use and develop and perfect our gifts. Instead, we run out and bury them in a grave of mediocrity and ultimate uselessness.

I just don't believe that God created us in his image to be mediocre people, fearful people. That isn't his will for our lives. Instead, buried deep within each of us is the desire to be whole and fulfilled. But so often feelings of insecurity and failure engulf us, and as a result we fall short of measuring up to what we know we ought to be. And when this happens, our God-given gifts atrophy; they become useless. We have failed through bad stewardship, and we suffer the pain that comes with our sin.

Happily, though, whether our hard times of

failure strike us because of some impetuous and un-
wise action or because we have buried our God-
given gifts and have failed to measure up to his
purpose for us, there is a sure remedy if we will
claim it.

The sure answer

Frederick Buechner, a gifted writer, says, "When
God speaks, things happen because the words of
God aren't just as good as his deeds, they are his
deeds. When God speaks his word, John says, creation happens, and when God speaks to his creation, what comes out is not ancient Hebrew or the
King James version or a sentiment suitable for fram-
ing in the pastor's study. On the contrary, 'The
word became flesh,' John says (1:14), and that
means that when God wanted to say what God is all
about, it wasn't a sound that emerged but a man.
Jesus was his name. He was dynamite. He was the
word of God."[1]

And it is this Jesus, this Dynamite, who will take
us through our hard times of failure and lead us into
personal fulfillment if we will act out the powerful
words found in Jeremiah 33:3, "Call unto me, and I
will answer thee, and show thee great and mighty
things" (KJV). And it is this same Jesus who said, "I
am come that they might have life, and that they
might have it more abundantly" (John 10:10, KJV).
There's no room for half-hearted mediocrity in these
words. Rather, they are powerful words of assurance that give us the courage to move through

life with zest and boldness—willing to risk even the possibility of failure, but always knowing that "If God be for us, who can be against us?"

But even as I've been writing this, my mind has wandered back over many years to the time in Louisville, Kentucky, when I was singing on the CBS network show "Greetings from Old Kentucky." Everything seemed to be going well, and I thought I was just great. But one day I read this comment by a *Variety* magazine critic, "The dull and drab vocalizing of Dale Evans did nothing to enhance the program." That was all he had to say about me—nothing more!

Outraged and heart-broken, I cried for a week, but then my Texas determination surfaced, and I vowed I would work hard. Someday I would "show him." Throughout the depression years of the 1930s there were times when I would sing for nothing over a little radio station located in the Chicago stockyards. Deep within me was the intense desire to sing—to use and perfect the God-given gift. Nothing else mattered then; I must sing!

So intent was I on the fulfillment of my dream that several years later when I was singing with the Anson Weeks Orchestra at the Cocoanut Grove on Wilshire Boulevard in Los Angeles and was offered a screen test by a Paramount Studio talent scout for an upcoming motion picture, I turned it down without a second thought. The offer was tempting, but I just had to make it as a singer.

Even during those years when I was ignoring the claims of the Lord on my life, I believed my talent for music was God-given, and I was determined to overcome every incident of failure. And then, of course, when I gave my life to him, recognition came which exceeded anything I could have dreamed of.

I like the way Robert Raines seems to sum up this whole idea with these words, "We are in charge of our lives. We can do great things. John Gardner says one of the reasons mature people stop learning is that they become less and less willing to risk failure. But without great risks there can be no great rewards. We can't ooze into the future. We have to leap into it."[2]

And leap into it we can, because as we surrender ourselves daily to God, life becomes all that it is "meant to be," and we can claim victory over every hard time, knowing that the "Eye hath not seen, nor ear heard, neither have entered into the heart of man, the things which God hath prepared for them that love him" (1 Cor. 2:9, KJV).

God in the Hard Times
of Temptation 5.

"The battle—our battle—against every temptation that can ever try to take us on has already been won on that first Easter morning. All we're involved in is a mopping up operation."

"Blessed is the man who endures temptation; for when he has been proved, he will receive the crown of life which the Lord has promised to those who love Him."

James 1:12, NKJV

"THE DEVIL MADE ME DO IT!"

Several years ago, this punch line, when tossed out casually by Flip Wilson, a popular comedian, after he had played a sly or dirty trick on someone, usually got a big laugh from the audience.

But I know from long and hard experience that the attacks of Satan are nothing to treat lightly or to laugh about. Quite the opposite, really. All of us have experienced our dark nights of the soul when we've been tempted to say or do something hurtful and then in a moment of weakness have given in to that temptation. As a matter of fact, the closer we try to walk with the Lord, the more difficult and intense these times are. And of one thing I'm sure—our help during those hard times of temptation does not come from blaming someone else, even the devil. He can tempt, but he can never make us do anything.

They are always with us

As Christians, we can be certain that each day will bring us a full quota of circumstances and events that will tempt us to be less than our best—to stretch or bend the truth, to spread a choice bit of gossip, to fudge here and give a little there, to flaunt our power, to put someone else down in order to look good ourselves, to substitute our personal gods for God. The list is endless. But if we allow our minds to dwell on the attacks of the Enemy and the raw and subtle temptations he sends our way in order to defeat our attempts to live in victory, we will then experience the bitter defeat that comes when we fail to draw on the resources that are ours. And when this happens, our witness as Christians is so defective it becomes almost meaningless.

But this is not God's will for our lives. He wants us to be all out Christians who, with his help, can handle the temptations that come our way. Dr. E. Stanley Jones told about a sign that was posted over the radiators in every room of a San Jose, California, hotel. It read, "Please turn the radiators all the way on or off. If turned partially on, they will leak and be noisy."[1]

What a graphic parable! When we're only partially turned on as Christians, we become "leaky and noisy." Our halfway spiritual life languishes and we are susceptible to temptation and its consequences—our powers of resistance are diminished.

The supreme example

The classic example for overcoming temptation is, of course, the story that Matthew, Mark, and Luke tell us about the temptations of Jesus in the wilderness of Judea as he began his public ministry. Each in his own way tells how Jesus left the dramatic and electrifying experience of his baptism east of the Jordan River and then walked into the desolation of the nearby wilderness west of the upper reaches of the Dead Sea. It was here in that arid, wild, and desolate wasteland that he was tested by Satan and subjected to three temptations: the temptation to misuse his powers and abilities . . . the temptation to show off and be a wonder-worker . . . the temptation to take a shortcut—to bypass the Cross as a means of reconciling us to God, of compromising with evil.[2]

There can be no doubt but that Jesus in those many days of being alone in that wild and desolate wilderness wrestled with each proposition that Satan laid on him. But had Jesus turned those stones into bread at Satan's seemingly innocent suggestion, it would have been a blatant misuse of his power for selfish purposes. If he had tried to impress the crowd by jumping off the top of the temple and landing safely 450 feet below in the Kidron Valley, they would have rushed after him as a wonder-worker without peer. And if Jesus had exchanged a few moments of worship of Satan in that secluded place where no one else could see for "all the kingdoms of the world," it would have meant that he had bypassed the Cross as the way of redemption— a shortcut not in God's plan. Jesus knew that evil couldn't overcome evil, so he stood firm, using the Word of God as his weapon in spiritual warfare.

We don't see a picture here in this awesome scene of a Jesus with a halfway turned on spirituality. Instead, he was bold and secure in his faith and confidence in God. And in that boldness and confidence he confronted his enemy with positive responses. God was with him during those long and lonely days of hard times and gave him the ammunition needed to overcome every vile suggestion. Here is our model for the 1980s! I like the promise in the way the writer of the Hebrews put it, ". . . because he has himself been through temptation he is able to help others who are tempted" (Heb. 2:18, JB).

There is no hint anywhere in this story that Jesus wavered for one minute. He didn't dillydally back and forth with the pros and cons of what was right and what was wrong—*he knew, and he acted.*

The Joseph saga

In the early pages of our Bible there is another classic story of how to meet temptation in a moment of crisis—the story of Joseph. Joseph was a virile and vigorous young man. As a teenager, he had been rejected by his jealous brothers and sold into slavery. His buyers then took him to the strange and faraway country of Egypt where no one knew him or his family or his God. There, through his talents and ingenuity, although still a slave, he in time became a trusted manager of the household of Potiphar, an official in the king's government.

But after a while he was confronted with a wrenching temptation for a young man—the sex-hungry and attractive mistress, Potiphar's wife, invited him to bed. But Joseph's commitment to God was so complete that he immediately drew on his spiritual resources and told her he could not commit that "great wickedness and sin against God."

She was persistent, though, in her seduction attempts, and finally one day when no one else was around, she grabbed his tunic and commanded him: "Sleep with me." To say that her approach was bold is an understatement, and at that moment Joseph knew there was just one thing to do—get away fast. So he slipped out of the tunic which she was still clutching tightly and ran out of the house. Then, in her fury at being rejected, Potiphar's wife accused Joseph of trying to attack her in her bedroom, and she displayed his tunic as evidence. Potiphar bought his wife's lie and threw Joseph into prison.

Compromise—secret sin—was not a part of Joseph's character. And while he served some prison time, God didn't forget him. Because of his refusal to knuckle under to temptation and his obedience to God, an amazing sequence of events occurred that ultimately put this astute young man in a place of national leadership second only to the king of Egypt.

David's blackest hour

Unfortunately, all of the Bible's temptation stories don't have happy endings, but we can learn even from these. Hundreds of years after Joseph's time David was firmly positioned as the mighty king of Israel. God had chosen him and blessed him in a marvelous way, and David molded Israel into a great world power. Throughout his rise to this lofty position David's integrity and his devotion to God had been above reproach.

But late one afternoon he walked out on his palace roof and looked down at the houses clustered below. On the roof of one he caught a movement, and as he looked closer, he saw a beautiful woman taking a bath. Why she chose to expose herself at this particular time, we don't know. Although, it is possible she knew it was David's habit to be out on the palace roof at that time each day. And why David didn't turn away from this enticing and seductive sight, we don't know. But it is obvious that he didn't. For instead of rejecting the temptation as Joseph had, David succumbed to it and sent a messenger to invite Bathsheba to his bedroom where she spent the night.

The story then moves to several weeks later when Bathsheba sends David a message that she is pregnant. Next begins the ignominious attempt at coverup which ultimately led to the death of Bathsheba's husband. And after that heinous act had been committed, she moved into David's palace and became one of his wives.

David's weakness at this time of temptation unleashed a sordid and tragic sequence of events which scarred his entire life. The depth of his anguish and despair is spelled out in the fifty-first Psalm for everyone to see as he cries out, "Have mercy on me, O God, according to thy steadfast love; according to thy abundant mercy blot out my transgressions. Wash me thoroughly from my iniquity, and cleanse me from my sin" (v. 1, RSV).

These words tell us the depth of David's feelings of remorse when the prophet Nathan confronted him with his sin. But unlike the conniving Bathsheba, David repented of his gross sin and received God's forgiveness. And the completeness of that forgiveness is affirmed many years later when, as David's long career drew to a close, the writer of Scripture says, "David son of Jesse was the man whom God made great, whom the God of Jacob chose to be king, and who was the composer of beautiful songs for Israel. These are David's last words: 'The spirit of the Lord speaks through me; his message is on my lips'" (2 Sam. 23:1–2, TEV).

Imagine! This was the David who was guilty of adultery and the murder of Uriah, Bathsheba's husband. The patience and forgiveness of God is beyond our ability to understand—even a little bit. Not that he is patient with our giving in to temptation and sin. But by his grace when this happens and when we repent and ask his forgiveness, he does forgive and will give us the strength and understanding to resist in the future.

Now, it may be quite easy for most of us as we sit in our urban and suburban comfort to be horribly judgmental of David's temptation and sin. And we may even feel very self-righteous when people around us get caught after giving in to the temptation to steal, cheat on one's wife or husband, be abusive—or whatever. Indeed, many of us tend to rationalize our behavior against a backdrop of "nicer" temptations.

The ego battle

For example, I've always fought a horrible battle with my ego—mine is as big as the Empire State Building in New York. A temptation that has plagued me is the desire to always be the star . . . to have the first and the last word . . . to get my opinion across because *I know* it is the "right"one . . . to be the center of attention at all times.

During my early years I was obsessed with the fanatical drive to be successful. Nothing salved my ego more than what I felt was a successful performance. I even believe the debilitating stage fright which plagued my every appearance was an inverted egocentric problem for me.

Happily, though, when I turned my life over to Jesus Christ and dedicated my talents to him, he delivered me from both my pathological success drive and my crippling stage fright. But since then I have continued to struggle with the temptation in my Christian concerts to "perform"—to put on a good show, to measure the impact of my witness by the length of the applause. And I still, at times, am tempted to feelings of inadequacy if on a program I follow someone whose music and spiritual impact has been, in "show biz" terms, dynamite. It is at such moments that I pray fervently to be used by God in whatever way he chooses, and I've leaned heavily on Paul's words, "I am crucified with Christ: nevertheless I live; yet not I, but Christ liveth in me; and the life which I now live in the flesh I live by the faith of the Son of God, who loved me, and gave himself for me" (Gal. 2:20, KJV).

I have come to believe as I've talked about this with others that one way or another we all are precariously susceptible to Satan's attack in the ego department of our lives. And we tend so often to glibly rationalize our ego excesses as harmless. Not so! They are insidious attacks which can bring defeat. But the answer to this problem is found in a moment-by-moment and day-by-day commitment of ourselves and our talents to Jesus.

I do want to emphasize, though, that there's nothing wrong with having a healthy ego. Actually, ego-strength is a God-given gift, but if and when it gets out of control, no matter how we rationalize the excess, we and other people will be hurt. An out-of-control ego is pure poison to a healthy and wholesome Christian life.

Now, I don't want to dwell here on the many very

personal temptations which plague all of us. But as I travel across this great land of ours and talk with people and listen to what they say, I am increasingly aware of two particular temptations that seem to be paralyzing the witness of so many Christians.

The temptation to be dull

Joy Davidman in her insightful book *Smoke on the Mountain* tells the amusing and yet rather sad story of a missionary who was attempting to convert an old African chief. In the course of the missionary's pleading and explanation, he had been dwelling heavily on the "thou shalt nots," and the old chief was paying close attention and listening carefully.

" 'I do not understand,' he said at last. 'You tell me that I must not take my neighbor's wife.'

" 'That's right,' said the missionary.

" 'Or his ivory, or his oxen.'

" 'Quite right.'

" 'And I must not dance the war dance and then ambush him on the trail and kill him.'

" 'Absolutely right!'

" 'But I cannot do any of those things!' said the savage regretfully. 'I'm too old. To be old and to be Christian, they are the same thing!' "[3]

For me, this story illustrates the picture that so many Christians present to the world today—we act old and sterile and juiceless and uninteresting, and we equate that style of life with being *Christian*. We concentrate on the thou-shalt-nots because we're deathly afraid to trust our freedom in the Lord. We are frequently seen by non-Christians—and even by some other Christians—as dull and humorless and dry . . . as if this world is a burden, something to be tolerated. So often we are repelling instead of compelling.

C. S. Lewis once told the story of the schoolboy who was asked what he thought God was like. "He replied that, as far as he could make out, God was 'the sort of person who is always snooping around to see if anyone is enjoying himself and then trying to stop it.' "4 What a tragic and distorted idea!

I think all of this is one of the most subtle temptations Satan lays on us today. After all, if this is what people outside of Christ really see when they look at us, we're not very attractive; we have nothing they want or think is important. In short, we don't represent or reflect a way of life that will give theirs zest and meaning. And so they turn both us and the gospel off.

How are we as Christians to handle this temptation of being dull and negative? Good question! Once again, though, I think we find our model in Jesus. Very early in the Gospel story Mark writes, "And as he sat at table in his house, many tax collectors and sinners were sitting with Jesus and his disciples; for there were many who followed him. And the Scribes of the Pharisees, when they saw that he was eating with sinners and tax collectors, said to his disciples, 'Why does he eat with tax collectors and sinners?' " (Mark 2:15–16, RSV). And over and over again we read that people were attracted to Jesus and followed him wherever he went. Luke even goes so far as to say that "all the people hung upon his words" (Luke 19:48, RSV).

Sinners and tax collectors . . . the crowds . . . all who hung upon his words—these were not attracted to a dull, super-pious, legalistic, negative, and uninteresting Jesus. I believe they were attracted to him because he was an exciting personality. They understood his language and were attracted by his actions. I just have to believe that he was fun to be around. After all, crowds don't follow a bore or an oddball. Jesus of Nazareth was a fascinating storyteller whose words were alive and warm. He didn't specialize in unintelligible religious jargon, and he cared deeply about people— all kinds and shapes of people. Wherever he went he breathed excitement. He lived his life, not on the edges, but in the center of events. He was no spectator but a zestful participant in what was going on. John has him saying, "I have come so that they may have life and have it to the full" (John 10:10, JB).

Roy and I take that statement of Jesus at face value—we love life; we want it "to the full." We've tried to learn from the model that Jesus gave us to be comfortable with all kinds of people, to be interesting ourselves. Don't misunderstand; we never want to compromise in our commitment to God. He knows our hearts and holds us steady, and, hopefully, our witness-door is open so that at all times we can communicate with today's "tax collectors and sinners."

"Right thinking" versus "right action"

A second and extremely subtle temptation which I believe is front and center in Satan's strategy to defeat us and blunt our witness is our tendency to make an idol out of "right thinking"—orthodoxy at the expense of right action.[5] We place a high premium on "right thinking," and, of course, that is good except that we are usually arrogant enough to interpret right thinking as *"our way* of thinking." Then we ride rough shod over anyone who doesn't agree with us.

The point is, though, that if Satan can get us to feel comfortable and satisfied that "our" thinking is "right," he can then lull us into substituting that for right action . . . or *no action at all.*

Dr. Paul Rees, one of America's leading pastors and mission leaders, phrased this idea so beautifully when he wrote, "Jesus was the Word really embodied; we are the Word rhetorically embalmed. Many of us . . . should cease to embalm the gospel in correct creed and begin to embody it in glowing deed."[6]

As a matter of fact, if the gospel is to reach people for Jesus Christ so that it makes a difference in their lives, both in this world and in the one to come, it can't be embalmed in "right thinking" or "creed" or in "verbal Christianity." Rather, it must be acted out in our person-to-person relationships on a day-to-day basis—in church, at the supermarket, in the privacy of our homes—wherever we are.

This is illustrated by the response Jesus gave to

the disciples of John the Baptist when they asked whether he was the Messiah or should they look for another. Jesus said, "Go and tell John what you have seen and heard: the blind receive their sight, the lame walk, lepers are cleansed, and the deaf hear, the dead are raised up, the poor have good news preached to them" (Luke 7:22, RSV). The proof was not just in what Jesus thought or in what he said. It was also in what he *did*—his actions in behalf of the poor, the sick, the blind, and the deaf.

Christianity is a *way of life*, not a laundry list of rules or right doctrine or conformity to a false pietistic style or possessing a vocabulary of impeccable and safe terms. It is being outraged by human suffering wherever people hurt . . . acting to relieve the poor, restore purpose to the frustrated, give presence to the lonely and all who feel left out and alienated. Christianity is not merely settling down to a comfortable routine. If lived according to the Jesus model, it involves restless and often uncomfortable living, a relentless pursuit of injustice in any form, and an openness to the risk and danger of really loving and caring for people at the expense of personal comfort and security.

The temptation to be comfortable . . . to be only halfway turned on . . . to be the star . . . to cheat on our income tax . . . to play sexual games . . . to put a rival down—to be less a person than God wants us to be—is to be involved in a frightening battle. In colorful language Paul warned the Christians in Ephesus, "Finally, grow strong in the Lord, with the strength of his power. Put God's armor on so as to be able to resist the devil's tactics. For it is not against human enemies that we have to struggle, but against the Sovereignties and the Powers who originate the darkness in this world, the spiritual army of evil in the heavens" (Eph. 6:10–12, JB).

But the battle—our battle—against every temptation that can ever try to take us on has already been won on that first Easter morning. All we're involved in is a mopping up operation. If we try to fight that "spiritual army of evil," we'll fail miserably and succumb to the subtleties of temptation. But when we throw the burden of our temptations on the Lord, we have the promise given to us by none other than David himself, "He shall sustain you; He shall never permit the righteous to be moved" (Ps. 55:22, NKJV).

God in the Hard Times of Success 6.

"Success is neither fame, wealth nor power; rather it is seeking, knowing, loving and obeying God. If you seek, you will know; if you know, you will love; if you love, you will obey."

Charles Malik

"If anyone wishes to walk in my footsteps, let him renounce self, take up his cross and follow me. For the man who chooses to save his life will lose it; while he that loses his life for my sake and the gospel's shall save it."

Mark 8:34–35, E.V. RIEU

"SUCCESS IS NEITHER fame, wealth nor power; rather it is seeking, knowing, loving and obeying God. If you seek, you will know; if you know, you will love; if you love, you will obey."

Dr. Charles Malik, former Lebanese ambassador to the United Nations, is responsible for this perceptive definition of success. It is one of the wisest and most profound statements I have ever read.

Now, it might seem strange to include a chapter in this book about God in the "hard times of success." Our natural tendency, even among Christians, is to believe that success of one kind or another would relieve us of all of our difficult times. We're convinced that if we could be just a little bit more suc-

95

cessful than we are, our problems would be solved and we would be sitting pretty. Oh, we may not say it that way in so many words, but in our day-to-day drive to "be somebody"—to be famous, to acquire the comfort of wealth, and to relish the sweet taste of power—we have allowed our values to become twisted and completely out of tune with the true spirit of Dr. Malik's description of success.

A success pilgrimage

I remember so well the thirst for fame that drove me relentlessly for many years from place to place as I struggled for recognition. There were times when it seemed as if recognition would never come. And then when I would get a break, something always happened, and I'd find myself out of a job. In my quest for fame and recognition I worked my way from one radio station to another, from one club to another. To sing and to act was more important to me than almost anything else. I wanted to be successful, to see my name on the marquee and headlined on top-rated shows.

Then one day, through the skill and contacts of my agent, Art Rush, a beautiful and gentle man, I landed an audition for one of the most popular radio shows of the 1940s, the "Chase and Sanborn Hour." On Sunday afternoon most of the radios in America were tuned into this NBC favorite, starring ventriloquist Edgar Bergen and his puppet, Charlie McCarthy. The show also featured popular actor Don Ameche and the Ray Noble Orchestra, one of the

finest in the Big Band era. Without question, Edgar
Bergen was one of the most talented performers of
the time. After all, to be successful and gain fame as
a ventriloquist on radio where the audience couldn't
even see what was going on required a special gift.

This was awesome stuff for a girl from Italy,
Texas, and I approached that audition with fear and
trembling. If I could get this job, I was sure my struggles and hard times would be over. The big day
arrived, and "I knew I had the job the minute that
crazy puppet Charlie McCarthy began whistling
through his wooden mouth. I smiled, Edgar Bergen
smiled, Art Rush smiled. A few days later I signed
the contract. . . . Professionally speaking I was
doing well again."[1] As the female vocalist for the
"Chase and Sanborn Hour" my voice could be
heard on radios from California to New York and
from Canada to Mexico. This was what I had struggled for and gone hungry for. I had arrived; Dale
Evans was now a success and famous.

A hollow victory

But the problems were still there. Underneath my
plastic show-business facade there was seething unrest. A battle was still raging below the surface because I was living a lie. At that time I couldn't even
admit publicly that little Tommy was my son for fear
it would destroy my show-business image. Mine
was a hollow victory, and I was living in a bubble
that was destined to burst. Burst it did, and it wasn't
until much later, after marrying Roy, that I turned

my life over to Jesus Christ and discovered that success was not to be found in fame but in serving God and witnessing to his saving power. And it was then that I was able to begin to identify in a small way with a truth discovered hundreds of years ago by Spanish mystic St. John of the Cross: "The soul makes greatest progress when it least thinks so, yes, most frequently when it thinks it is losing ground. The soul makes greatest progress when it travels in the dark, not knowing the way."

But there is precious little of the spirit of Dr. Malik or St. John of the Cross in so much of our drive for achievement . . . to make a name for ourselves . . . to be famous . . . to be super-Christians . . . to build the biggest Sunday school or church in our city or state or country . . . to be a part of the biggest or the most prestigious denomination. Now, don't get me wrong. I believe God wants us to be effective witnesses to his love and grace. But somehow I have the uneasy feeling that we live such breathless lives in the midst of the massive human traffic jam which makes up our lifestyle that our sense of being and meaning are out of step with the true spirit of Christ.

The Jesus answer

One day Jesus stood in the middle of a crowd of people and gave them some pretty straight talk on this subject. He said, "If anyone wishes to walk in my footsteps, let him renounce self, take up his cross and follow me. For the man who chooses to save his life will lose it; while he that loses his life for my sake and the gospel's shall save it" (Mark 8:34–35, E.V. RIEU).

There's no hint in these words of striving to be famous, to be number one, to be the best or the biggest or the showiest. On that black crucifixion day Jesus was neither famous nor successful to the people who watched that procession along the Via Dolorosa to Calvary or to those who witnessed the brutal execution. They viewed him as infamous not famous, as a failure, not a success.

But all of that began to change three days later on that glorious Resurrection morning and in the days that followed. I'm sure those disciples of Jesus remembered well his earlier words passed along to us by Mark in the light of what happened. No longer did they see themselves as favored subjects of an earthly king who would throw off the yoke of their Roman oppressors. No longer were they obsessed with who would sit on his right hand or his left. They were beginning to understand Christ-like values and priorities.

William Barclay, that well-known interpreter of the Bible for, as he used to say, "the common man," spelled out the true Christ-life in these words: "God gave us life to spend and not to keep. If we live carefully, always thinking first of our own profit, ease, comfort, security, if our sole aim is to make life as long and as trouble-free as possible, if we will make no effort except for ourselves, we are losing life all the time. But if we spend life for others, if we forget health and time and wealth and comfort in our desire to do something for Jesus and for the men for whom Christ died, we are winning life all the time."[2]

But, to use Dr. Barclay's phrase, "winning life all the time" does not give us insurance against hard times. It may well be in God's plan for each of us in our own way to experience a degree of success and fame within our small circle of friends or in our profession or in our town or even in our country. In fact, I somehow believe he wants that for us. But the big question is: Can he trust us to remain firm in our Christian convictions when the inevitable hard times threaten to tear us apart?

Success is not fame

Among those who have achieved success and a degree of fame in our country today is Senator Mark Hatfield of Oregon. Senator Hatfield is a beautiful Christian gentleman who readily admits that any honest politician possesses a strong measure of ego and ambition in order to succeed. His pilgrimage from the Oregon State Legislature to Senior Senator from the state of Oregon has filled many years of public service. He has tasted the recognition and fame that comes from being a member of the "most exclusive club in the world"—the United States Senate. Yet Senator Hatfield has remained firm in his Christian stand even during some very dark days and troubled times. He writes, "Radical allegiance to Jesus Christ transforms one's entire perspective on political reality. Priorities become totally changed; a whole new understanding of what is truly important bursts forth."[3]

Roy and I have been mightily blest of God. He has permitted us to experience a measure of success—yes, even of so-called fame as western personalities. Through it all we have tried to remain faithful to our Lord. But we're both intensely human, and there have been times of testing that were outrageously hard—times when everything seemed dark and foreboding. But I am here to bear witness to the fact that at such moments we have turned again and again to God's Word and found the strength we needed. Frequently, we have claimed that marvelous promise expressed by the prophet, "I have chosen you and have not rejected you. So do not fear, for I am with you; do not be dismayed, for I am your God. I will strengthen you and help you; I will uphold you with my righteous right hand" (Isa. 41:9–10, NIV).

Success is not wealth

No, success is not fame, and turning back to Dr. Malik's definition, nor is it wealth. Now, most of us in these days of inflation and high taxes are convinced that we don't have a problem with wealth. But don't you believe it! To the vast majority of the people living in the world today we—you and I—are wealthy. To the dirt farmer, the coffee picker, and the cane cutter in Third World countries, we are rich.

This fact was driven home to me some years ago

when I was in Haiti. There I saw, as I traveled for World Vision International, the extremes of poverty. There I saw babies with stomachs bloated from malnutrition and agonizing mothers and fathers who spent all of their waking hours trying to scratch out a living from the tired and arid soil in an effort to feed themselves and their children. To them, $500 a year would be wealth. But such horror stories make us painfully uncomfortable. How the heart of God must ache when he hears our complaints about bills and the high cost of living!

Yes, we are a society of wealthy people, but wealth is not success. Wealth—the having of things—will not free us from undergoing hard times—times of stress, of loneliness, of discouragement, of heartache. But again, if our hearts are tender and open to the promises of God, if our intentions and attitudes are sensitive to good stewardship, we can be confident that he will sustain us and enrich our lives.

In our Gospel stories is a tale of two men—two "successful" men, two wealthy men. One is a model of final failure. The other is remembered for his devotion, compassion, and honor.

The first was a successful farmer, and it wasn't easy to grow good crops in first-century Palestine. But he had learned his profession well. He had worked hard and managed his investment carefully and was doubtlessly well-respected in his community.

Over a succession of years crops had been good, and he had the foresight to build large storage barns. Here indeed was a man who gave every appearance of wisely handling his affairs. In today's world this fellow would likely be elected to the city council or the state legislature or even to congress. In all probability he would have been a pillar in the church and chairman of the finance committee.

But as time passes, the story takes on a peculiar twist. Apparently, he got fat and lazy and self-centered—spiritually and intellectually obese. Like many of us, he had the habit of talking to himself, and one day he said, "You have plenty of good things laid up for many years. Take life easy; eat, drink and be merry" (Luke 12:19, NIV).

What a shriveled up old man he had become! Now he was ready to shut out the rest of the world with its hunger and poverty and injustice and retreat into the security of his own acreage—inside his own high fences—and take life easy, interrupted only by an occasional round of dinners and parties.

But his reverie is broken into by the awesome voice of God, "You fool! This very night your life will be demanded from you. Then who will get what you have prepared for yourself?" (Luke 12:20, NIV).

This story is usually referred to as "The Parable of the Rich Fool." Jesus told it to illustrate a point: the lasting values in life are not wrapped up in the abundance of possessions. At the same time there is no hint in this story that God condemned this man because he was rich—because he had an abundance of things. Rather, he was a fool because of his sick and distorted values. And this can happen to us whether our income is $5,000 a year or $500,000.

The second man, Joseph, was a wealthy and honorable person from the little town of Arimathea, probably located fifteen or so miles northwest of Jerusalem in the foothills. We know very little about him except that in addition to being described as good and honorable and rich, John says he was a secret disciple of Jesus. But each of the four Gospel storytellers mentions him and describes briefly the scene that has given him unforgettable recognition in Christian history.

On the day of Jesus' infamous execution by the Roman soldiers, it was Joseph who courageously shed his cloak of secrecy and went to see Pilate, the Roman procurator of Judea, and asked for the body of Jesus. Then, for whatever reason, Pilate granted his request, and Joseph, along with Nicodemus, took the body of Jesus down from the cross and gave him an honorable burial in Joseph's unused tomb in the garden.

This is all we know for sure about Joseph, although tradition suggests that he became influential as a Christian leader and headed a group of Jesus' followers who preached the gospel in Britain, where he died and was buried. But Joseph's story is in sharp contrast to the one told earlier by Jesus about the "rich fool." Joseph's single act of devotion in selflessly burying Jesus in what was probably a family tomb marks him as a man with a healthy set of values which determined his wise use of wealth.

Joseph's success, which brought him wealth, shines across history like a beacon light off the rugged coast of New England and is a twentieth-century model for us. Whatever the wealth of our abundance we dare not relax and become comfortable and self-satisfied when even today thousands of people are living in poverty in the streets and alleys of lower eastside New York. Instead, like Joseph from the little town of Arimathea, our calling is to use wisely what we have as a means of reaching the lost and ministering to them for Christ in very practical ways.

But even good stewardship will not prevent our experiencing difficult times. Our success in overcoming those hard times, though, is assured through the words the Lord gave Moses when Israel looked ahead to the difficulties they would face as they moved into the Promised Land: "Be strong, stand firm, have no fear of them, no terror, for Yahweh your God is going with you; he will not fail you or desert you" (Deut. 31:6, JB).

Success is not power

Perhaps one of the most subtle forms of success that plagues all of us is seen in our striving for power within the confines of our own little worlds. Dr. Malik recognized this, too, in his statement at the beginning of this chapter—and for good reasons.

It is true that probably most of us would shrug our shoulders and say this doesn't apply to our situation. Don't you believe it! Consciously or unconsciously, a struggle for power goes on all the time— between a husband and wife in the home . . . between parents and children . . . on the job, in the store, or in the office . . . in church and on church committees . . . on the golf course and in all competitive sports . . . within our social circle of friends and acquaintances.

Unfortunately, thirst for power spills over all too frequently into our church life. We jockey for position on influential committees so as to get our way. Our urge to be a part of the "in" group, to be seen with the "right" people, is often nothing more than an ill-disguised effort for a position that will enable us to exert power and bend events in the directions that suit *our* purposes. And as we become convinced that to us alone has been given the pattern for the kingdom of God on earth, we often maneuver and manipulate people and events under a pious cloak of defending the faith.

But this is not new. Human nature has remained pretty much the same for over two thousand years at least. This is seen as we recall the story of Jesus and his disciples climbing the road from the Jordan to Jerusalem just a short time before that fatal week that ended with the crucifixion and the first day of the glorious new week that began with the Resurrection morning. As the disciples tagged along behind Jesus on that rugged and dusty road, they were "apprehensive," "bewildered," "dismayed." Jesus had tried to prepare them for the dark days ahead, but they didn't and wouldn't understand.

Instead, the disciples and others with them were caught up in their own ambitions and worries and concerns. They weren't unified in the common cause of following Jesus and helping other people—

not at all. They were a self-seeking and ambitious group. Each of them wanted his own way—a place of power and importance in Jesus' kingdom.

It was in this setting and mood that James and John edged up to Jesus and said, "Master, we want you to do for us whatever we ask." How is that for a selfish request? And still, so many of our prayers today have that same ring!

Then when Jesus asked them what they wanted, their reply was, "Let us sit one on your right hand and one at your left, in your triumph" (Mark 10:35–37, GOODSPEED). They wanted a place of prominence and influence at his triumph—when he came into power. David McKenna comments on this scene: "A power struggle threatens to destroy all the work that Jesus has done to weld the Twelve into a unified, working body. He has to nip the rebellion in the bud. Calling the Twelve together, Jesus talks to them about the standard which the Gentiles use to determine greatness. Touching on the tender spot of men who have been ground under the heel of Roman oppression, Jesus reminds them of the Gentile rulers who use their power to 'lord it over' them."[4]

Jesus knew that any form of striving for success through power crippled the personality and the human spirit. So he went on to tell them that anyone who achieved greatness and power of any kind must take on the role of serving and being helpful to people. And this was indeed a universal message which applies equally to us today in the church, in our neighborhoods and clubs, in Christian organizations, in every place where we touch the lives of people.

A twentieth-century model

The twentieth century has given us a magnificent model in the life of Gandhi of a person who used power as a means of serving people. It has been said of him that "his politics were intertwined with the practical, day-to-day problems of the millions. His was not a loyalty to abstractions; it was a loyalty to living, human beings."[5]

At the age of forty-six Gandhi returned to India from South Africa with one purpose—to free his country from foreign domination. Over the following years his popularity and greatness grew. But he also endured hard times that go way beyond our ability to comprehend. He was beaten, suffered indignities, imprisoned. He fasted almost to the point of death. Yet he didn't give in to the misuse of his popularity and power or compromise his principle of non-violent civil disobedience. Instead, as expressed by an Indian sage of his day, "He had the marvelous spiritual power to turn ordinary men around him into heroes and martyrs."

Hard times? Gandhi knew them. But as he was struck by the bullets from an assassin's gun, he uttered one word: "Rama," the Indian word for God—and then he died.

The Daniel model

But perhaps one of the most colorful examples we can find anywhere of the point Jesus was trying to get across to his disciples on the Jerusalem road is found in the person of Daniel—one of the most highly principled and godly men in our Bible story. Unfortunately, most of us have grown up with a rather childish view of this great man as we have seen him only as the hero of the little song "Dare to Be a Daniel" and in the saga of Daniel in the lion's den. But Daniel's greatness ran very deep.

Peggy Stanton, in her marvelous book titled *The Daniel Dilemma*, summarizes Daniel's life: "In the Old Testament, the story of Daniel is the story of man's relationship to power and the Creator of power. The Bible describes Daniel as a man of great gifts; fair of face and form, keen of intellect, possessed of wisdom and understanding. His natural endowments keep him continually in the company of kings; all of whom consult him as to the meaning of their dreams. The dreams center on one basic message. The king's authority exists only by a grant from God. If the kings abuse their power, it will be taken away from them. As a result of Daniel's ability to translate the kings' visions, he is made the ruler of Babylon. But, unlike the kings, he never forgets the source of his power. When he is forced to make a choice between King Darius and God, he chooses God, knowing the choice will land him in the lion's den.

"There are many morals in the saga of Daniel, but one is particularly obvious. Daniel's faithfulness to God did not remove pressure from his life. It sometimes increased it. Daniel was always engaged in the use of power. He was frequently challenged to abuse it in order to retain it. But never did Daniel defect to mere earthly authority. Never when his power was taken away, as in the lion's den, did he cease trusting God. As a result, he always survived circumstance."[6]

As Mrs. Stanton has said so well, "Daniel's faithfulness to God did not remove pressure from his life." In fact, few people have experienced the crises of hard times as did this amazing man. But he had learned well the message of the Psalmist, "Cast thy burden upon the Lord, and he shall sustain thee: he shall never suffer the righteous to be moved" (Ps. 55:22, KJV).

Senator Hatfield sums it all up for us, "Our call is to faithfulness, not to efficacy; it is to servanthood rather than power. We know that the most decisive action that we can take to shape history is to follow the way of Christ, to give ourselves to the building of the Body, and to pour ourselves out as he did in love."[7]

God in the Hard Times
of Marriage 7.

"Married life is one of God's greatest gifts. It isn't a time for settling down but for growth, for doing new things. With each passing year a growing couple will actively look for new and different things they can do together . . . new hobbies . . . new friends . . . new ideas to think through . . . new projects to undertake . . . new places to see and enjoy. It takes planned effort and work. None of this will happen by accident; it comes through careful and loving planning . . ."

Love is "slow to lose
patience. . . . Love has good
manners. . . . It is not
touchy. . . . Love knows no limit
to its endurance, no end to its
trust, no fading of its hope; it can
outlast anything. Love never
fails."

1 Corinthians 13:4–7, PHILLIPS

———————————————————

"A LOVING MARRIAGE is as much a miracle as the parting of the Red Sea."

I'm not quite sure about the origin of that statement, but when you stop to think about it, that is just a whole lot more than a witty comment. We're all familiar with the gloomy statistics that clutter up newspaper and magazine articles today about the current epidemic of marriage failure. And that is sad. But equally tragic is the large number of marriages, even among Christians, that are intact but not really happy or loving. And this tragedy is all the more sad when we realize that at one time those unhappy people had stars in their eyes and love in their hearts. Once there was a surge of romance that

113

swept them along like the Mississippi River at flood time.

Our start

It has been almost thirty-six years, but my heart still skips a beat when I remember the night that Roy proposed to me. We had been working together for some time in motion pictures, on radio, and in personal appearances. In late 1947 we were booked for a number of rodeo shows across the country. One night we were waiting to go on in the cavernous Chicago Stadium which was jammed to the rafters with an enthusiastic and expectant crowd. We were decked out in colorful western regalia and sitting astride horses that were straining to gallop out into the arena and the spotlights. I had the jitters and knots in my stomach that always preceded a show. We'd been making the usual small talk, when suddenly I heard Roy ask, "What are your plans for New Year's Eve?"

That seemed like a funny question to pop just a few moments before going into our act, but I answered, "I don't have any plans."

Then to my amazement he said, "Fine. Why don't we get married then?" He had no more than gotten those words out of his mouth when the announcer called out our names and Roy charged off to the center of the arena waving his hat to the crowd. I didn't have time to do anything but gulp before I galloped in behind him to the cheering of thousands of people. Believe it or not, I had to go through our entire act before I could give my answer.

Of course, the answer was yes. And on December 31, 1947, with an Oklahoma blizzard raging outside, Roy and I looked into each other's eyes and promised our love for the rest of our lives. That's the way we started.

But there's more. On the second night of our honeymoon my ever-loving new husband came up with the idea that this would be a "great night for coon hunting."

I had been proposed to while sitting on horseback in the Chicago Stadium, married in a blizzard, and just one night later there I was trudging around in the snow-covered and frigid Oklahoma countryside. Our musical accompaniment that night was the baying of the coon dogs and the whistle of wind through the trees. Shivering with cold and teeth chattering, I remembered that I'd said "for better or worse," but I couldn't recall anything about coon hunting!

We returned to Southern California in a fever-pitch of excitement and were immediately plunged into the flurry of combining two families into one home. We were mature enough to know there would be some rough times ahead. I'd been living with the inner fear that Roy's children wouldn't accept me as their stepmother, and it wasn't long until difficulties did surface. But we all worked hard at it, and with the help of the dear Lord we came through with flying colors.

Commitment prevails

Believe me, though, ours is not a "they rode off into the sunset and lived happily ever after" story. It has been almost thirty-six years since our wedding night in that Oklahoma blizzard and the coon hunt. There have been other storms that have rocked our marriage, and we have been through some desperately hard times as we've been devastated by the tragic death of three of our children.

In our struggles to shape a happy and lasting marriage we've failed each other and God many times when our egos clashed and we've been less than our best. But we have made it a rule never to let misunderstandings fester "until the boil bursts." And through it all our commitment to each other has held steady, and our faith in God has kept us on track. So often we've turned to the words the Lord gave Paul in one of his hard times, "My grace is enough for you: my power is at its best in weakness" (2 Cor. 12:9, JB). And there has been plenty of weakness!

It has helped to realize, though, that no two people can come together in marriage out of different backgrounds and values without experiencing hard times. And it is certainly unrealistic to assume that two completely different personalities can blend together on a day-to-day basis without going through some very real and crippling difficulties. But I feel that if both persons in a marriage *want* to make it work, a miracle as great as the parting of the waters of the Red Sea for the Israelites at the time of the

Exodus can happen if there is commitment to each other and to God.

In their book *Long-Term Marriage*, Floyd and Harriett Thatcher highlight the importance of commitment with this thought: "Our own experience underlines the idea that commitment within the marriage relationship transcends and goes beyond feeling; it is a decision, consciously made. It is a decision—a choice—made by two people in love in the deepest meaning of the word; it is not merely an expression of love symbolized by saying 'I do' before a minister or judge. Rather, it is an authentic love acted out on a daily basis toward one's spouse."[1]

Feelings are not enough

I believe the point made here is terribly important. Yes, feelings are important—we are people with feelings. God made us that way. Our emotions are God-given. But it is essential for us to understand that in our humanness our feelings can change from hour to hour and from day to day. There are times, though, that commitment in marriage goes beyond feelings and becomes an act of the will. We *will* to affirm and express our love even in our hard times.

If we are honest about it, there are times in marriage when we don't *feel* very loving or in love. Disagreements and hurt feelings can easily snarl our relationship. Such things as misunderstandings over money or the disciplining of children or the pressures of work can open up rifts in the marriage. And so often in the heat of those disagreements harsh words are spoken and things are said that cut deeply. Feelings of love change to anger and hostility, and if these are allowed to fester, a slow poison develops, *feelings* of love are blunted. But it is in such moments that true commitment holds us steady, and as Christians, we grab hold of such promises and admonitions as the Apostle Paul gave us when he wrote, "Let all bitterness, and wrath, and anger, and clamour, and evil speaking, be put away from you, with all malice: And be ye kind one to another, tenderhearted, forgiving one another, even as God for Christ's sake hath forgiven you" (Eph. 4:31–32, KJV).

Believe me, I know from long experience that when two caring people who are committed to each other wrestle with the inevitable hard times that confront every married couple in a spirit of *kindness* and *tenderness* and *forgiveness*, miracles do happen.

No place for boredom

Then, too, I have been utterly amazed to discover as I have talked with people in my travels that so many marriages are unhappy because of boredom. This has surprised me because it is not something I've experienced in my own life and marriage to Roy. But I have thought a lot about it and can see how easily this can happen.

In one of his books, Dr. Paul Tournier, a prominent Swiss psychiatrist, validates this idea when he writes, "I once heard Dr. Theodore Bovet, a specialist in marriage problems, remark that the worst enemy of marriage was plain boredom."[2] Then Dr. Tournier goes on to explain his agreement with that statement.

And, of course, boredom is deadly in any kind of a relationship, but this has got to be especially true when it afflicts a married couple. Over and over again, I've asked myself and others just how this can happen. What causes hard times of boredom in marriage? How can such times be avoided? And what can we do about it if and when it happens to us?

I recall so well the fever-pitch of excitement I felt and the high expectations I had when Roy and I were married on that cold December night in 1947. But such feelings are common to most married couples. So what can happen after two, five, ten, or twenty years of marriage to dull those feelings?

Ruth, an attractive woman in her early forties expressed it this way, "When Ben and I were married, we were very much in love. Every day was a new adventure. Then after a year and a half I got pregnant. We were thrilled and looked forward eagerly to the coming of our baby. And when our little daughter was born, we just felt like we had the world by the tail. Times weren't easy from a financial point of view, but we took it all in stride.

"But as the years passed Ben became completely absorbed in his work, leaving home for the office sometimes as early as seven in the morning, and more often than not he didn't get home until eight or nine o'clock at night. Most of the time he was too tired to even talk much, and after an hour or so of relaxing before the television set, he usually headed off to bed.

"When our little Beth was old enough to go to school, I took a job to fill my time and soon settled down to a routine of my own. Every week day was pretty much the same. And then on Saturdays I was busy catching up on work around the house and doing the necessary shopping. Ben would work in the yard and around the house all day. By Saturday night we were both exhausted—too tired to go out for dinner or anything else.

"Sunday morning we slept as late as possible but still made it to Sunday school and church. And most of Sunday afternoon was spent sprawled out before the television set or sleeping. That's the way we lived day after day, week after week, and month after month. We never went anywhere or did anything new and exciting, and we never seemed to have much to talk about on a deep level.

"Over the years we've drifted apart emotionally. We'll probably stick it out and grow old together, but there's no excitement in our marriage. It's dull and I'm bored to death."

That is not what God intends for any two people! Jesus said that he expected us to have "life in its fullness" (John 10:10, PHILLIPS). Our birthright in Jesus Christ is a life filled with energy and excitement and adventure. Yes, we all have our routines—our highs and our lows—but there is no room for boredom if our spirits are in tune with God and the adventure of living.

The "settling down" trap

But what about Ruth and Ben? Where did they go wrong?

Naturally, there's no one answer to those questions. But I think at least part of the answer is that they got married, had a baby, and *settled down*. On the surface that sounds all right. But I wonder if a lot of marriages are not wrecked by *settling down*, by slipping into dull routines, by getting too comfortable with one another, by taking each other for granted, by never doing anything new and different together, by not growing as persons and as a couple.

Married life is one of God's greatest gifts. It isn't a time for settling down but for growth, for doing new and exciting things. With each passing year a growing couple will actively look for new and different things they can do together . . . new hobbies . . . new friends . . . new ideas to think through . . . new projects to undertake . . . new places to see and enjoy. It takes planned effort and work. None of this will happen by accident; it comes through careful and loving planning, together and separately. But the rewards are well worth the effort—each new day brings fresh adventure when we look for it and expect it. That is what Jesus meant about living life in its fullness.

Now, don't misunderstand me; I know we live in a real world. There's none of the Pollyanna in me. In our humanness we may all slide into hard times of boredom now and then. It is unrealistic to think that any two people will live on the mountaintop all of the time. But I firmly believe that if we come to every new day and every new stage in life with an attitude of expectancy and of excitement, God will meet us in our difficult moments and gently guide us to new experiences of adventure.

The communication trap

Let's go back to Ruth and Ben one more time. Toward the end of Ruth's dreary lament she said something terribly important, "We never seemed to have much to talk about on a deep level."

According to professional people who devote their time to studying the marriage relationship, comparatively few young married couples really talk with each other on a deep and feeling level, and it doesn't seem to get any better in the long term. This isn't to say they don't communicate with each other at all, but for the most part their talking moments are filled with nothing but small talk.

David and Vera Mace, a couple who have given most of their lives to marriage enrichment, point out that poor communication is the basic cause of hard times in marriage. Apparently, though, there is a widespread notion "that married couples have no particular difficulty in communicating with each other. That is true enough if we confine communication to passing on information. Where couples get into trouble is in communicating their *feelings*, both positive and negative, to each other. We now know that two people can on outward appearance live close together, yet inwardly be living in quite different and separate worlds. Only when they are open to each other's deepest thoughts, feelings, and intentions can they really live a shared life."[3]

A shared life! I think this is the secret to overcoming hard times of poor communication in marriage. And I have to believe this is what God intended, for we read in both Genesis and Ephesians that God's marriage pattern is: "They two shall be one flesh"; "the two will become one" (Eph. 5:31, TEV).

What a beautiful description of intimacy in marriage! And it is this kind of intimacy that gets beyond the superficial "passing of information" to that deep level where we truly share our feelings. But for most of us this kind of communication doesn't come easy.

No, it isn't easy for two people to "become one"—even for two people in love. After all, each person comes from different backgrounds, spiritually and socially. Each partner in a marriage sees and expresses things differently based on particular family and cultural backgrounds. And as a result of these differences, our communication lines get fouled up and misunderstandings and hurt feelings emerge. Harsh words are spoken in anger or we pout and retreat behind a high wall of silence. What started out as a comparatively insignificant misunderstanding grows until it becomes a major issue and carries a potential for further explosions or the deathly silence of a cold war.

While it is true that every married couple experiences the beginnings of such scenes, it is at those very moments—those hard times—when God wants to meet us. And *he will* with such reminders as love is "slow to lose patience. . . . Love has good manners. . . . It is not touchy. . . . Love knows no limit to its endurance, no end to its trust, no fading of its hope; it can outlast anything. Love never fails" (1 Cor. 13:4–7, PHILLIPS). You'll notice—I said God "wants to meet us." He does! But he won't overrule our thoughtlessness or our stubbornness. He has to be invited to participate in those hard times with us.

Yes, I believe "love never fails" if two people want it to last—and it takes two people to communicate effectively. Both must want to communicate out of deep feelings of love and caring. But communication is a two-way street. It requires sending and receiving. And, unfortunately, most of us are so busy broadcasting that we fail to really receive—to listen. We may *hear*, but much of the time we don't *listen* to each other.

Shared togetherness

I like the way Dr. Paul Tournier expresses this: "It is impossible to overemphasize the immense need humans have to be really listened to, to be taken seriously, to be understood. No one can develop freely in this world and find a full life without feeling understood by at least one person."[4] And certainly, one's husband or wife should be that "one person" if marriage is to become that exciting and growing adventure God intends it to be.

Each of us longs to be affirmed, to be loved, to be accepted, to be able to communicate on a feeling level with our husband or wife. But to be affirmed, we must be affirming and not critical. We must love if we want to be loved, to accept if we want to be accepted.

But these shared moments of intimacy must be planned for. Many couples I know have a specific time every day that is uniquely theirs. These are times for *talking with* and *listening to* each other. And it is in these moments of shared togetherness that we express our needs, our hopes, our fears—yes, and our love.

The Hosea story

One of the most remarkable men in our Old Testament story was a great prophet in Israel who lived in the eighth century B.C. His name was Hosea. He lived in some pretty dark days. There was a great deal of political instability in his times. There were wars and rumors of wars. At the same time Israel, in spite of her glorious past, had pretty much conformed to the culture of the surrounding countries. What worship of God that still prevailed was blended in with worship of other gods, and there has even been the hint that cultic prostitution might have seeped into their lifestyle. It was a seamy picture.

There is a great deal of speculation about Hosea and his story, but in putting the bits and pieces together, we can be certain that he was a strong nonconformist. Prophets in those precarious days had to be rugged men—men of nerve. But we do know also that Hosea was a very sensitive person, for he was obviously moved by the evidence of an awesome God who was graphically seen in the wonders of nature around him.

But our interest here is in his marriage. In fact, almost at the beginning of Hosea's story we read of his marriage to Gomer. It is likely that at first this was a happy marriage that produced two sons and a daughter. But then hard times fell on their relationship. Gomer was apparently seduced by the sexual immorality that had penetrated Israel's society, and she left Hosea and their three children. Details of her life right after that are sparse, but we do know that ultimately, out of either necessity or desire, she sold herself and became a slave and probably a concubine.

It was then that Hosea, in response to the urging of the Lord and out of a heart of love and compassion, redeemed Gomer from her life of slavery and sin by paying her owner fifteen silver shekels and a bushel and a half of barley, and they were reunited again. With loving care Hosea began the tender process of restoring their relationship—even as he went on to serve the God of Israel against the heavy odds of opposition.

Now, Hosea was a flesh and blood man—a man of passion and of integrity. The agony of his experience must have been excruciating. His feelings of rejection and despair had to be intense. But God was with him in those hard times.

The footprints mystery

In 1981 at the Presidential Prayer Breakfast in Washington, D.C., President Reagan told a deeply moving story which came to him from an anonymous source that illustrates well the love and sustaining power of God as we confront our moments of difficulty and pain.

One night a man dreamed that he was walking with the Lord in the sand at the seashore. As they plodded along together to the sound of the pounding surf, the man became aware of the fact that a succession of scenes was being reflected in the sky above him. One after another he saw pictured there each event and experience of his life. And then as the final scene faded away, he turned and looked back down the beach. As his eyes swept the distance, he saw stretched out behind him two sets of footprints, but here and there along the way only one set of footprints was visible—his. As he pondered this strange sight, he realized that whenever a particular hard or low time in his life had appeared in the sky only one set of footprints was visible.

Turning to the Lord, he said, "When I turned my life over to you, you said that if I would walk with you, I would never be alone—you would always be with me. Why did you desert me in my times of greatest need?"

The Lord replied, "I didn't desert you. When you saw only one set of footprints, it was then that I carried you."

During any of our hard times, I believe we can count on the Lord to carry us. But I also believe this was especially true for Hosea during his moments of tragedy when he was deserted by Gomer. And it applies equally to us as we work through the hard times in our marriage relationship.

God in the Hard Times of Death 8.

"Three times Roy and I have felt the painful laceration of death as we stood, crushed, by the graveside of our children. To call these 'hard times' seems the understatement of the century. These were intensely human moments for me. . . . But even in the midst of my pain I knew somehow that God stood near in my lonely walk 'through the valley of the shadow of death' and that his 'goodness and mercy' were with me forever."

"Even though I walk
    through the valley of the shadow of death,
I will fear no evil,
    for you are with me;
your rod and your staff,
    they comfort me."

Psalm 23, NIV

"I HATE TO TELL you this," he said, "but as a doctor it is my obligation. Robin's heart has undergone considerable strain. It may not be able to stand the strain much longer. I can't tell you exactly what will happen or when it will take place, but it might be a good idea for you and Roy to prepare yourselves."[1]

Our beloved little two-year-old "angel unȧ vare" was deathly ill. Mumps complicated by encephalitis had caused her fever to skyrocket until it reached her brain. It was more than her frail and handicapped body could handle, and just twenty-four hours after the doctor's warning, we heard the nurse's whispered words, "She's gone."

§ § §

"The moment I pulled into the driveway I knew something was wrong. Our housekeeper, Ruth Miner, came out to meet me.

"Taking me by the arm, she said, 'Dale, the bus had an accident after it left San Diego. Debbie and Joanne Russell are with the Lord.'

"With the Lord? For a split second it failed to sink in. Then the realization struck like a blow from a hammer. She was telling me that Debbie was dead; beautiful, fun-loving, full-of-life Debbie had been killed in an accident."[2]

§   §   §

"We drove out to Forest Lawn Cemetery and walked into the Church of the Recessional. Here we had said 'goodbye' to Robin and to Debbie; here, now, was the flag-draped casket of our Sandy. There was a service, mercifully short, and we followed him out through the doorway to the churchyard. A military escort walked ahead of us; a bugler blew 'Taps,' and from the rifles of the escort there cracked out a sharp salute . . .

"The flag was taken from his casket, folded in the traditional ceremony, and handed to me, his mother. I held it to my heart, and then we turned away, and left him with God."[3]

§   §   §

Three times Roy and I have felt the painful laceration of death as we stood, crushed, by the graveside of our children. To call these "hard times" seems the understatement of the century. These were intensely human moments for me. The deep hurt seared through my body like a rampaging forest fire in our California mountains. But even in the midst of my pain I knew somehow that God stood near in my lonely walk "through the valley of the shadow of death" and that his "goodness and mercy" were with me and would stay with me forever.

Death—a daily reality

But even as I recall, and in a sense relive, the deaths of my three children, my wonderful mother and father, my only brother, my much loved grandfather and grandmother, and other family members and friends over the years, I am keenly aware that every moment of every day persons are struggling through the pain and loneliness that ravages the heart when a loved one is taken by death.

Television news reports from the Middle East and Central America flash vivid scenes of violent death and moving grief into our living rooms every day. And all too often our composure is shattered by the death of someone closer at hand—a tragic and senseless accident . . . a victim of crippling disease . . . the suddenness of a heart attack with no warning . . . the peaceful slipping away of one in advanced years.

But however and whenever it happens, we're never really ready for the trauma of the human separation we know as death. And it is in such moments that we shout, "Why? I don't understand, God! It is so wrong." Then following the storm comes those still, tear-filled moments when, if we are Christians and sensitive to the voice of the Lord, we hear the voice which whispers the sure promise, "My grace is sufficient . . ." And while we don't understand, we can accept because, with Saint Augustine, we know that "If divine truth were not too large for our understanding, it would be too small for our hearts."

God's ways are not our ways

But every once in a while I hear someone say something that really bothers me. In fact, this was brought to mind recently when a woman called a radio talk show and told how "the Lord took" her little four-year-old girl who had died of leukemia. Now, I think I know what she meant, but somehow I just don't believe that the Lord "takes" our loved ones, and I know of more than one unbeliever for whom this idea has been a stumbling block.

It is true, though, that all of us are subject to the laws of sin and death that have been a part of our world since our first parents disobeyed God. As such, the consequences of ever-present evil are with us. And it is equally true that God has given us and all people everywhere the freedom of choice—to choose good or evil . . . to hurt or to heal.

I hurry to say, though, that I believe God *accepted* our Robin and Debbie and Sandy when they were taken from us by death because they were his. And in God's overall and mysterious purpose for all of our lives we have to believe that his eternal will has somehow been done. But then, that is where we have to let it rest because I don't believe it is possible for us in this life to ever comprehend God or to understand his ways.

Madeleine L'Engle, a most insightful writer, expresses it well when she says, "The only God who seems to me to be worth believing in is impossible for mortal man to understand, and therefore he teaches us through the impossible." She goes on to say that she feels there may be the tendency on the part of some Christians today to want "to make God possible, to make him comprehensible to the naked intellect, domesticate him so that he's easy to believe in. Every century the church makes a fresh attempt to make Christianity acceptable. But an acceptable Christianity is not Christian; a comprehensible God is no more than an idol."[4]

Ours is not a comprehensible God. And this idea is validated by that majestic yet very earthy Old Testament prophet when he passed along those words of wisdom we all need to hear in our black moments of questioning and confusion, "For my thoughts are not your thoughts, neither are your ways my ways, says the Lord. For as the heavens are higher than the earth, so are my ways higher than your ways and my thoughts than your thoughts" (Isa. 55:8–9, RSV).

A lasting hope

Roy and I have gained strength to endure the hard times of death because we knew that God was not only near, he was with us. This truth is beautifully illustrated by Mrs. Charles E. Cowman in her heart-warming little book entitled *Handfuls of Purpose:* "There is a fascinating legend concerning a tribe of North American Indians who roamed in the neighborhood of Niagara. Each year they offered a young virgin as a sacrifice to the Spirit of the Mighty River. She was called 'The Bride of the Falls.'

"The lot fell one year to a beautiful girl who was the only daughter of an old chieftain. The news was carried to him while he was sitting in his tent; but on hearing it, the old man went on smoking his old pipe in complete silence.

"On the day set aside for the sacrifice, a white canoe, full of ripe fruit and decked with flowers, was ready and waiting for 'The Bride.' At the appointed hour she took her place in the frail bark. It was pushed out into midstream where it would be carried swiftly toward the mighty cataract.

"Suddenly, to the amazement of the breathless crowd, a second canoe was seen to dart out from the river bank—in it was seated the old chieftain. He paddled with swift and powerful strokes toward the swirling sacrificial canoe. He reached it, gripped it firmly, and held it fast.

"The eyes of the father and daughter met in one last look of love; and then, close together, they were carried by the racing current until they plunged over the thundering cataract and perished side by side.

"The father is 'IN IT' with his child."[5]

136

Jesus feels grief

One of the most touching stories in the New Testament is passed along to us by John, the beloved disciple of Jesus. It is the story of three special friends of Jesus—two sisters and their brother, Mary, Martha, and Lazarus.

Word came to Jesus one day that Lazarus, his dear friend, was deathly ill. But upon his arrival at the outskirts of Bethany, Jesus was told that Lazarus had been dead and buried four days. Then, as he moved on toward the home of his friends, Martha, who had been forewarned of his arrival, hurried out to meet him. They talked briefly, and yet in those few short moments Jesus made one of his most profound statements—words of assurance and promise that have given hope to millions in the centuries since, "I am the resurrection and the life; he who believes in me, though he die, yet shall he live, and whoever lives and believes in me shall never die" (John 11:25–26, RSV).

Next, the story tells us that Martha hurried back to the house well ahead of Jesus and told Mary he was on the way. Without waiting for him to arrive, Mary rushed out down the street to meet him. And when she saw Jesus, the dam holding back her grief broke.

When Jesus saw the depth of Mary's pain, he was "deeply moved in spirit and troubled," and then John, in telling the story, describes the Master's reactions in two poignant words, "Jesus wept." As with the Indian chieftain and his daughter in the story of "The Bride of the Falls," Jesus was "IN IT" with Mary and Martha!

Never alone

There can be no minimizing of the pain, the devastation, the terrible feeling of loss, and the loneliness that comes with the death of a husband or of a wife or of a child—any loved one, relative, or friend. These are hard times that can really be understood only by one who has experienced them. But I can assure you that there are no shortcuts through the grieving process. At the same time, though, I can also testify to the fact that we never have to go through them alone. For one of the greatest truths of the gospel was expressed by our Lord when he said, "I am with you always."

We are never alone!

And that promise was made real on the first Easter morning, when after three days in the grave following that black crucifixion Friday, Jesus conquered death for all time as he walked out of Joseph's tomb. Jesus was alive. He *is* alive!

Dr. James McCord captured the drama within our hope when he wrote, "Easter . . . is that overwhelming awareness of the presence of God coursing through our day-to-day struggle to maintain a home, raise children, earn a living, and get along reasonably well with family and neighbors. It represents the triumph of light over darkness, freedom from emotional despair . . . life over death."[6]

Eternal victory

Another great Christian of our time, Dr. Helmut Thielicke, beautifully expresses the hope that is ours as we confront the hard times of death when he writes, "As the Easter stories report, a hole has been torn in death's door: Jesus could not be held by its chains. Upon this certainty were all the Gospels written, and the light of Easter now reflects back upon the events of the life of Jesus, illuminating them anew and in another perspective than that available to Jesus' companions and contemporaries. Easter . . . is the key to everything."[7]

As a matter of fact, it was the drama of that first Resurrection morning that changed completely those fearful disciples, who had run in terror for cover at his death, into bold and Spirit-intoxicated witnesses of Jesus in the days that followed his return to heaven. They came to understand that "neither death nor life . . . can ever come between us and the love of God made visible in Christ Jesus our Lord" (Rom. 8:38–39, JB). And they became *Resurrection Christians* who moved out boldly across the world with the good news that Jesus is always with us—even in our hardest moments of separation and loneliness and death.

In the very closing words of our Bible we have the final promise passed along to us by the Beloved Apostle when he wrote, "Behold the dwelling of

God is with men. He will dwell with them . . . he will wipe away every tear from their eyes, and death shall be no more . . ." (Rev. 21:3–4, RSV).

Death shall be no more. It is this declarative promise that has kept me from being bitter and resentful during those paralyzing moments when we've had to confront the hard times of death. And it is this promise that can open up the way for every child of God to mature and grow and learn as we move through this life toward that glad day when we will be united with our loved ones in the glory made available to us through Jesus Christ. For it is not in our strength that we endure life's hard times—but in his strength.

Perhaps no words of Scripture have touched so many hearts during life's darkest moments as has the twenty-third Psalm. It was my mother's favorite, and she died while it was being read to her. It has sustained countless children of God in their hard times. It will give us healing and strength and hope when we most need it . . .

> The Lord is my shepherd, I shall lack nothing.
>   He makes me lie down in green pastures,
> he leads me beside quiet waters,
>   he restores my soul.
> He guides me in paths of righteousness
>   for his name's sake.
> Even though I walk
>   through the valley of the shadow of death,
> I will fear no evil,
>   for you are with me;
> your rod and your staff,
>   they comfort me.

You prepare a table before me
   in the presence of my enemies.
You annoint my head with oil;
   my cup overflows.
Surely goodness and love will follow me
   all the days of my life,
and I will dwell in the house of the Lord
   forever.

(Ps. 23, ɴɪᴠ)

About the Authors

DALE EVANS ROGERS is the author of eighteen books, virtually all of them best-sellers. She has pursued successful careers as a recording artist and a TV and motion-picture personality. On New Year's Day, 1977, Dale and her husband Roy shared the honor of being Grand Marshals of the Tournament of Roses Parade. In addition, she has made more than 5,000 appearances for charities in behalf of abused, orphaned, and retarded children. One of America's most honored and beloved women, Dale Evans Rogers is the recipient of the highest awards from numerous organizations, including the American Legion, the American Bible Society, the National Film Society, and the National Committee for the Prevention of Child Abuse.

FLOYD THATCHER has been involved in management and editorial roles in Christian publishing for more than thirty-six years, fifteen years of which were with Word Books, Publisher, as Vice-President and Editorial Director, until his retirement in 1982. He presently serves as part-time Editor-in-Chief of Word Books in addition to writing and lecturing and teaching writing. Floyd is coauthor, writer, and editor/compiler of seven previous books, including *Long-Term Marriage*, which was written with his wife Harriett. And he has lectured widely on written communication at various conferences at universities, colleges, and seminaries.

Notes

Chapter One

1. Henri J. M. Nouwen, *Reaching Out* (Garden City, N.Y.: Doubleday and Co., Inc., 1975), 19.

Chapter Two

1. Robert A. Raines, *To Kiss the Joy* (Waco, Tex.: Word Books, Publisher, 1973), 23–24.

Chapter Three

1. Richard J. Foster, *Celebration of Discipline* (San Francisco: Harper and Row Publishers, 1978), 13.
2. Eugene Kennedy, *A Time for Love* (New York: Doubleday and Co., Inc., 1970), 30.

Chapter Four

1. Frederick Buechner, *Peculiar Treasures* (San Francisco: Harper and Row Publishers, 1979), 72.
2. Raines, *To Kiss the Joy*, 29.

Chapter Five

1. E. Stanley Jones, *Mastery* (Nashville: Abingdon Press, MCMLV), 87.
2. Myron Augsburger, *Matthew*, The Communicator's Commentary, vol. 1 (Waco, Tex.: Word Books, Publisher, 1983), 50.
3. Joy Davidman, *Smoke on the Mountain* (Philadelphia: Westminster Press, 1953, 1954), 13.
4. C. S. Lewis, *Mere Christianity* (New York: Macmillan Publishing Co., 1964), 69–71.

5. G. C. Berkouwer, "Orthodoxy and Orthopraxis," in *God and the Good*, ed. Clifton Orlebeke and Lewis Smedes (Grand Rapids: Eerdmans, 1975), 13–21.
6. Paul S. Rees, "Lift Up Your Eyes," *World Vision*, September 1976, 23.

Chapter Six

1. Roy Rogers and Dale Evans with Carlton Stowers, *Happy Trails* (Waco, Tex.: Word Books, Publisher, 1979), 107.
2. William Barclay, *The Gospel of Mark* (Philadelphia: Westminster Press, 1975), 205.
3. Mark O. Hatfield, *Between a Rock and a Hard Place* (Waco, Tex.: Word Books, Publisher, 1976), 27.
4. David L. McKenna, *Mark*, The Communicator's Commentary, vol. 2 (Waco, Tex.: Word Books, Publisher, 1982), 218.
5. Louis Untermeyer, *Makers of the Modern World* (New York: Simon and Schuster, 1955), 395.
6. Peggy Stanton, *The Daniel Dilemma* (Waco, Tex.: Word Books, Publisher, 1978), 9.
7. Hatfield, *Between Rock and Place*, 217.

Chapter Seven

1. Floyd and Harriett Thatcher, *Long-Term Marriage* (Waco, Tex.: Word Books, Publisher, 1980), 56.
2. Paul Tournier, *The Meaning of Persons* (New York: Harper and Row Publishers, 1957), 35.
3. David and Vera Mace, *Marriage Enrichment in the Church* (Nashville: Broadman Press, 1976), 39.
4. Paul Tournier, *To Understand Each Other* (Atlanta: John Knox Press, 1967), 8.

Chapter Eight

1. Rogers and Evans, *Happy Trails*, 158–59.
2. Ibid., 191.

3. Dale Evans Rogers, *Salute to Sandy* (Old Tappan, N.J.: Fleming H. Revell Co., 1967), 109–10.
4. Madeleine L'Engle, *The Irrational Seasons* (New York: Seabury Press, 1977), 19.
5. Mrs. Charles E. Cowman, *Handfuls of Purpose* (Los Angeles: Cowman Publications, Inc., 1955), 109–11.
6. Floyd Thatcher, *The Miracle of Easter* (Waco, Tex.: Word Books, Publisher, 1980), 102.
7. Helmut Thielicke, *The Faith Letters* (Waco, Tex.: Word Books, Publisher, 1978), 157.

7-4